# LUCKY
# **IRON**
# FISH

# LUCKY IRON FISH

## A Social Enterprise
## Tackling Iron Deficiency

Gavin Armstrong
and Herb Shoveller

DUNDURN
PRESS

Publisher: Kwame Scott Fraser | Acquiring editor: Kathryn Lane | Editor: Olga Filina
Cover designer: Karen Alexiou
Cover image: fruits: Monstar Studio/shutterstock.com; fish: Courtesy of LIFe.

**Library and Archives Canada Cataloguing in Publication**

Title: Lucky iron fish : a social enterprise tackling iron deficiency / Gavin Armstrong and Herb Shoveller.
Names: Armstrong, Gavin (Founder of Lucky Iron Fish Enterprise), author. | Shoveller, Herb, author.
Description: Includes index.
Identifiers: Canadiana (print) 20230473458 | Canadiana (ebook) 20230473504 | ISBN 9781459752481 (softcover) | ISBN 9781459752504 (EPUB) | ISBN 9781459752498 (PDF)
Subjects: LCSH: Social entrepreneurship—Southeast Asia. | LCSH: Iron deficiency anemia—Southeast Asia—Prevention.
Classification: LCC HD60.5.A785 A76 2023 | DDC 338/.040959—dc23

We acknowledge the support of the Canada Council for the Arts and the Ontario Arts Council for our publishing program. We also acknowledge the financial support of the Government of Ontario, through the Ontario Book Publishing Tax Credit and Ontario Creates, and the Government of Canada.

Printed and bound in Canada.

Dundurn Press
1382 Queen Street East
Toronto, Ontario, Canada M4L 1C9
dundurn.com, @dundurnpress ✖ f ⊙

*This book is dedicated to the people of Cambodia. With their kindness and support we have been able to bring the Luck of the Fish around the world. Thank you for welcoming us into the Kingdom of Wonder.*

# Contents

*The following is the story of the Lucky Iron Fish journey told through its founder Gavin Armstrong. Herb Shoveller combined the Armstrong discussions with other interviews he conducted and crafted all of those stories into this book.*

# Chapter 1

# Origins of Lucky Iron Fish

YOU HAVE SEEN the photos and video clips. Impoverished children, some with distended bellies, and sad, dark eyes who lack basic, healthy food. Then there are the parents, in particular mothers, who are desperate to keep their little ones healthy and safe while attending to their own at-risk health.

This reality was particularly poignant for Drs. Christopher Charles and Gavin Armstrong, whose health-related research while at the University of Guelph in Canada brought them into close contact with the South Asian country of Cambodia and its people.

Cumulatively the pair spent years conducting research on dietary challenges in the mostly landlocked country, whose lush beauty awed them. One of its rich, if not richest, natural resources is the Mekong River, which is the leading source of the people's mainly pescatarian, or fish, diet. Though just getting by with severely limited resources, these people were always willing to share what little they had with their foreign guests.

Through their work, both researchers came to admire and care for their Cambodian hosts, who projected a warmth, friendliness, and generosity toward their foreign guests that belied their strictly limited economic means.

In return for such welcoming kindness, Charles and Armstrong were determined to use their work to find ways to improve the health outcomes for these people, especially children and women, in this beautiful land that they themselves had come to love.

The challenge is that such goals are difficult to attain for millions and millions of people, in particular in low- to middle-income countries. What happens to those malnourished children? Aside from having limited food, they lack energy, their mental faculties suffer, and their education lags behind where it should be.

A devastating period of political upheaval in Cambodia made such challenges even worse. Much of this story is influenced by that upheaval, which culminated in four years of genocidal rule by the Khmer Rouge, led by Pol Pot, between 1975 and 1979. Even before that devastating period there was turmoil in the country.

In fact, the turmoil in Cambodia began eight years before the Khmer Rouge took power after a bloody civil war. As a study from the University of Minnesota recounts, "The war pitted the Cambodian monarchy, and later the Cambodian Republic, and its allies, including the United States, against the Cambodian communists. The communists received support from the neighboring Vietcong."

The country's monarchy, while revered in some cases for advancing nationalism and loyalty, was also burdened by charges of corruption. As a result of that ineffective governance, several groups were united in trying to overthrow the monarchy. In an ironic twist, those groups included both right-wing and leftist groups as allies, and one of the groups on the left was the Khmer Rouge.

Underpinning much of the unrest through the civil war was massive income inequality where "Cambodians living in the urban areas enjoyed relative wealth and comfort while the majority of Cambodians toiled on farms in the rural communities. This obvious division of class made Cambodia especially susceptible to revolution," the University of Minnesota analysis explains.

The Cambodian genocide, over those four years of Khmer Rouge rule, was characterized by intense violence that saw between 1.5 and 3 million people killed at the hands of the Khmer Rouge, the Minnesota study outlines, which accounted for about one-quarter of the country's population.

The genocide was the result of a social engineering project by the Khmer Rouge, in which they were attempting to create a classless agrarian society. The Khmer Rouge sought "a radical reorganization of Cambodian society. This meant the forced removal of city dwellers into the countryside, where they would be forced to work as farmers, digging canals and tending to crops. Gross mismanagement of the country's economy led to shortages of food and medicine, and untold numbers of people succumbed to disease and starvation."

The Khmer Rouge regime eventually collapsed when Vietnam invaded and sustained an occupation for more than a decade.

Given the Khmer Rouge's focus was on a rural agrarian society, those "considered an intellectual were targeted for special treatment. This meant teachers, lawyers, doctors and clergy were the targets of the regime. Even people wearing glasses were the target of Pol Pot's reign of terror," the Minnesota research explains. To this day, even more than four decades later, older Cambodians who lived through that terror and need glasses still refuse to wear them.

As the principals in our story will recount, the warm and hospitable Cambodian people they came to care for deeply still harbour that fear, and the economic ramifications are still being felt by the relatively impoverished population, including health and diet challenges such as iron deficiency anemia.

In the end, Pol Pot evaded capture and was even able to wield power under the radar for many years.

"When the United Nations Transitional Authority in Cambodia [UNTAC] came to the country in 1992, it engaged Pol Pot and the

Khmer Rouge as a necessary partner to bring peace to Cambodia," the Minnesota study explains. "One of UNTAC's stated goals was to bring Pol Pot and other senior Khmer Rouge officials to trial. However, Pol Pot would die in 1998, before the trials took place." The years of civil war, Khmer Rouge brutality, and Vietnamese occupation left deep scars on the souls and bodies of Cambodians. Among those scars, and for our discussion here, the seemingly endless burden of poverty leaves people vulnerable to illness and disease, including iron deficiency anemia. Such health challenges are particularly acute in countries like Cambodia and are the focus of a range of international bodies and organizations trying to deal with the problem.

"Diets that don't provide the right levels of vitamins and minerals can compromise your immune system, impair your cognition and school performance, decrease your work productivity. This is a widespread problem, impacting individuals, families, and communities everywhere in the world, although particularly in lower-income countries," Lynnette Neufeld, director of the Food and Nutrition Division at the Food and Agriculture Organization of the United Nations (FAO), explained in a recent article.

Micronutrient deficiencies are highest in lower-income countries because diets often lack the diversity of nutrient-rich foods and tend to derive a large share of their calories from rice, wheat, maize, or similar staple foods. In fact, studies have concluded that nine in ten women in several countries in South Asia and sub-Saharan Africa are nutrient deficient. Though perhaps not as severe or common, deficiencies can also be surprisingly high even in higher-income countries.

Diets that don't provide the necessary levels of vitamins and minerals can compromise immune systems and impair cognition, as well as lead to dizziness, decrease work productivity, and cause low birth rates, and they may contribute to risks of non-communicable diseases. A key culprit in this sad drama is iron deficiency anemia.

"I had worked with some women who had been part of interventions through other NGOs [non-government organizations] many years ago, and during their pregnancies they had been offered a supply of iron pills," explains Charles, who did groundbreaking research on iron deficiency in Cambodia. "It was amazing, because they could clearly identify that after they started taking an iron supplement how much better they felt. They said that they had more energy, they felt stronger, they could think more clearly. Then, after the pregnancy, their supply of iron pills ran out and over the following months, that fog, those same sorts of feelings, returned. They felt like they were slowly being drained of energy and slowly losing their ability to concentrate."

Ironically, despite the widespread impact of micronutrient problems such as iron deficiency, there are clear solutions. According to Saskia Osendarp, executive director of the Micronutrient Forum, people need to have access to a range of micronutrient-dense foods, such as animal-source foods, dark green leafy vegetables, and beans, lentils, or peas. Health programs can provide supplements to those with extra needs, such as pregnant women and malnourished children. And food fortification can help make up the difference when healthy diets are unaffordable or inaccessible.

Food fortification is the practice of adding vitamins and minerals to commonly consumed foods during processing to increase their nutritional value. This is the aim of Lucky Iron Fish Enterprise (LIFe) as we will learn over the course of this story.

According to the non-profit Borgen Project, which points out the effectiveness of the Lucky Iron Fish, malnutrition can cause iron deficiency anemia, which happens when someone doesn't have enough iron in their blood. It is estimated that the condition affects 30 percent of the population globally. Armstrong, building on Charles's seminal design, worked on evolving a small, fish-shaped iron implement into a commercially viable social enterprise.

Originally conceived to address the high malnutrition rates in Cambodia, the concept continued to expand to become a significant player in the supplements industry on a growing global basis. The fish is simply dropped into boiling liquid, such as soup or water for rice, for ten minutes, and it releases a significant proportion of the daily recommended iron.

To gain a deeper insight into the signs, causes, and effects of iron deficiency, we can turn to observations shared by the widely revered Mayo Clinic based in the U.S.

The clinic says:

> Iron deficiency anemia is a condition in which blood lacks adequate healthy red blood cells which carry oxygen to the body's tissues. If lacking sufficient iron, the body can't produce enough of a substance in red blood cells that enables them to carry oxygen which, for example, could leave people tired and short of breath.
>
> Iron deficiency anemia may sometimes go unnoticed, but as deficiency worsens, the symptoms of anemia intensify. Common signs and symptoms include extreme fatigue, weakness, pale skin, chest pain, fast heartbeat or shortness of breath, headache, dizziness or light-headedness, cold hands and feet, inflammation or soreness of your tongue, and brittle nails and poor appetite, especially in infants and children with iron deficiency anemia.
>
> While iron deficiency anemia can affect anyone, there are groups who are at a higher risk. One group is women of child-bearing age because they lose blood during menstruation, putting them at greater risk of iron deficiency anemia. Infants and

children also have higher vulnerability. Infants who don't get enough iron from breast milk or formula may be at risk because children need extra iron during growth spurts. The surest way to manage that risk is to ensure children have a healthy, varied diet. In addition, individuals who don't eat meat, such as vegetarians, can be at risk if they don't have other iron-rich foods. Frequent blood donors should also closely monitor their iron reserves.

Complications can occur if iron deficiency becomes severe, and this can be especially acute in lower-income regions, such as Cambodia. In pregnant women, severe iron deficiency anemia has been linked to premature births and low-birth-weight babies, but supplements, such as that provided by Lucky Iron Fish, can help mitigate this outcome. And in infants and children, severe iron deficiency anemia can lead to delayed growth and development and increased susceptibility to infections.

A story Armstrong offers by way of example took place in Guatemala, which also demonstrates the growing global impact of Lucky Iron Fish.

"This one has stood out to me, where a mother said she was really sad because she wanted to walk her daughter to school but wasn't able to because after doing all of her jobs in the morning, she felt quite tired," he recalls. "She was dizzy, she had headaches and was just very fatigued. But then she was given an iron fish through an NGO and after a few months, she was able to regain enough energy every day to walk her daughter to school. She said it was because of the iron fish that she was finally able to do that."

That mother passed that story on to the NGO, which shared it with the Lucky Iron Fish team.

There are clear steps to prevent iron deficiency anemia by choosing iron-rich foods, yet in lower-income parts of the world this is often not an option, which again points to the value of supplements such as that offered by Lucky Iron Fish. Examples of iron-rich foods include red meat, pork, poultry, seafood, beans, dark green leafy vegetables such as spinach, dried fruit such as raisins and apricots, iron-fortified cereals, breads, pastas, and peas. Such nutritious foods are not necessarily easy to source in lower-income parts of the world.

To prevent iron deficiency anemia in infants, babies should be fed breast milk or iron-fortified formula for the first year, though this is a simpler solution in developed nations as opposed to lower-income regions where mothers themselves may be iron deficient.

"One story that sticks out in my memory was a fascinating one about a remarkable woman," Armstrong recalls. "In Cambodia, there are community leaders that are elected for each commune, and at one that we were at, one of those leaders was a woman and at that time there were not a ton of women elected to this role. She was certainly a minority.

"As a woman in that role, women's health issues were really important [to her]. She said she had suffered from bouts of weariness and didn't realize the likely cause at the time, but it was almost certainly low iron. She was interested in the iron fish, but she didn't want to recommend it to the community until she used it herself. So the NGO in the community at the time gave her a fish and she began to use it. And after a period of time she said, 'You know, this actually works, I feel better. I'm not dizzy, I don't have headaches.'

"As a result, she then felt able to recommend the fish to the community. That was just a demonstration of great leadership, being willing to be the test subject, essentially, for her community."

It became clear for Armstrong from the above case that women should be involved in making decisions on women's health, because they're closest to what is happening with food preparation and the challenges of raising children in many lower-income regions.

"I mean, this was a powerful image of this woman in charge in that village and why we need more women in charge of such matters," Armstrong stresses.

Armstrong and Charles were motivated to help the people of Cambodia because they recognized the lasting impact of the Khmer Rouge regime and they were confident their work could improve people's lives.

"There is a book I was given when I moved to Cambodia called *Cambodia's Curse*, and it talks about that dark chapter of their history," Armstrong explains. "There are people who are still alive who experienced life under the Khmer Rouge. You still kind of see the impact of that trauma on the population.

"I recognize that trauma can be generational, but you see this country with people who are so kind and everyone displays smiles and happiness, but the history is so dark and so recent. I think that is great motivation for people to want to do good there. And it's why I think a lot of people fall in love with the country because people are so kind even though they've come through such hardship."

One of the impacts of those treacherous years is caution around trust. The reluctance of some to wear glasses is an example. Another example is how important it was for the woman village elder mentioned above to experiment on herself first before recommending the iron fish to the community.

The trauma of the Pol Pot years, in Armstrong's assessment, can still be seen in the way its impact, and the wariness to trust it engenders, trickles down to malnutrition and iron deficiency issues in Cambodia.

"I just think it's a region where there is a stark difference between those who have income and those who are living on sort of impoverished wages that are about a dollar a day," Armstrong assesses.

"The issue is particularly acute in rural areas. And it's quite a rural country. There's a lot of garment production there which means low-paying jobs in factories that make major fashion brands. I think it just falls into that trap that many lower-income countries fall into. I think it boils down to sustenance farming and low-paying jobs."

Armstrong says that when visitors spend time in these rural communities, they witness endless examples of lethargy and general tiredness.

"It's sheer exhaustion," Armstrong describes. "And the mothers are usually cooking, and they've got multiple kids around that are climbing on them and playing at their feet. But they have to prepare the family meals, so they just try to power through. But they are so tired."

And then there are cultural considerations as well. For example, if there is not enough money in the household, the men get the food first because they are the ones working in the fields. That means if there's not enough food at the end of the day, the women are out of luck, or they get smaller portions. Those circumstances, in Armstrong's experience, merely compound the probability of iron deficiency.

"They're malnourished when they're not getting a full meal as well. That's the sort of generational gender disparity that exists all over."

While the visible effects of malnutrition and iron deficiency were ever-present, the baseline for the core work into the Lucky Iron Fish had to be the research, the blood testing. For one thing, there would be cases of the placebo effect, where individuals would think they were drinking iron-fortified beverages and would say, "Oh, I feel better, it's great."

Users believed they could feel the benefits right away, even though clinically it would take three to six months. This belief helped maintain the high compliance rates.

Armstrong explains that the research teams stayed away from the communities where research was going on, to control against conflicts of interest or bias. The teams relied heavily on the quantitative data from blood testing.

Still, the on-the-ground stories were telling.

"There are examples of mothers telling us that their kids are doing better in school, that they're not as sick, they are not falling asleep in class," Armstrong says. "There was a lot of this anecdotal information."

But the quantitative data would ultimately tell the scientific truth.

# Chapter 2

# Christopher Charles and the Groundbreaking Research

CHRISTOPHER CHARLES WAS an undergraduate student at the University of Guelph in Canada when he came to a life-changing realization: he vastly preferred research to standard classwork and exams. Now an anesthesiologist based in Barrie, Ontario, Charles always found joy in unearthing the unknown and solving problems to help others, characteristics that would serve him well as he ventured into rural Cambodia in 2008. It was a trip of discovery and, ultimately, the initial stages in the evolution of Lucky Iron Fish.

From the relative comfort of Guelph, Charles was thrust into a new world. He was living in a traditional Cambodian hut called a Phteah Keung, with local scientist couple Nary and Tharith, who were tasked with helping him identify health issues experienced by people in the area. There was no running water or electricity, and Charles would bathe by the river. He was a new, distinct face in a place that had never had a westerner as a resident before. Nary and Tharith would translate for him as he tried to adjust to a very different life than he was accustomed to.

"It was a learning opportunity for all of us," says Charles. "Their English was elementary at the start and my Cambodian was non-existent. We reached a point where their English and my Cambodian got better, and we were able to communicate effectively as time went on.

"I spent the first month or two going around to different communities that surrounded the village I was living in. I would talk to families, mostly women, about their health, concerns that they were able to self-identify, and how they were managing."

Charles had spent the previous couple years of his bachelor's degree in the lab, sprinkling in some fascinating summer jobs that enabled him to travel the world and work in an area of personal interest, the field of global health. As he neared the end of undergrad, Charles was in search of a way to combine that passion for research and health work.

"I always thought I would go into medicine," he adds.

On his path to med school, however, Charles was first contemplating doing a master's degree. He began applying for government funding and was successful in landing federal money to work in Cambodia. Charles connected with Heather Murphy, a Ph.D. engineering candidate at the time who was completing work on water and sanitation in the Asian country. She had directed him to a reputable water and sanitation–centric NGO named Resource Development International — Cambodia. He began to research the issues facing the Cambodian population and found that helminth (parasitic worms) infections were pervasive. Hookworm infections, as they are more commonly known, were a result of poor water conditions and caused both malnutrition and anemia. Another cause of anemia is iron deficiency.

Charles planned to go to Cambodia for three months after he had completed his bachelor's degree and before his master's. But the project soon grew bigger when he realized the extent of the problems in the region. The best national estimates at the time suggested that anemia affected 50 to 60 percent of the population, which Charles recognized as a staggering number. After carefully designing some studies, he was finding that closer to 92 to 95 percent of the population was testing anemic.

"There was no government intervention," notes Charles. "It was tough to see. To go out and collect these narratives from people and to have conversations about how they felt, their energy levels, and how they were going to get through their day was difficult. They were literally ticking off every single sign and symptom of anemia that you would find in a textbook. That was the reality for these people. Their quality of life was so impacted by anemia. It was a big challenge."

When he was out and about, Charles would visit pharmacies, or at least what passed as pharmacies, always on the lookout for iron pills to assess the supply, the cost, and so forth. His sobering discovery was that iron pills were unattainable for families. In almost all cases, households would bring in perhaps a dollar or two a day, while a one-month supply of the pills could range from $2.50 to $7.50, and that was just for one person. So the pills were simply out of reach for families with several children and other adults in the household.

"My initial work was to try to quantify the prevalence of anemia in those communities. At the end of the three-month period, I realized that I had collected this huge swath of data and uncovered a massive problem. I was going to hand the project off and maybe it would sit on someone's desk and perhaps that would be the end of it."

Charles was in a psychological and moral crisis. He had a decision to make. Ultimately, he called his adviser at the University of Guelph, Dr. Alastair Summerlee, who was also serving as the school's president at the time, and expressed his concern that he couldn't just walk away from these Cambodian people in need. He wanted to delay his master's to do more work overseas. Summerlee, whom Charles describes as a "big thinker, flexible, and an intellectual powerhouse," got back to his future graduate student with a proposal — stay in Cambodia and focus the master's on global health rather than lab-bench research.

"That seemed to tick a lot of boxes," says Charles. "Pretty quickly, things changed course."

With a new life plan, Charles was energized to do the important work in Cambodia and take steps to help resolve some of the health issues of these people whom he was getting to know and care for. He did weeks of research and found a series of anthropological studies from the 1970s set in sub-Saharan Africa and Brazil that examined the use of iron cooking vessels in anemia prevention. Initial findings usually suggested that using iron cookware on a regular basis had a positive effect.

"The concept is that if you're cooking in an iron pot, some of that iron will leach from the pot, go into the food, and enrich it," notes Charles. "Even if you're eating an iron-deficient diet, you're able to provide that little bit of supplementation at the household level.

"But the problem with iron cookware is that it's not widely used in the developing world. It's very costly and heavy. Families will leave food in cooking pots and if leftovers sit overnight, the food absorbs more iron, altering the taste and colour.

"I ran with the idea and thought, 'What if there was a way to add iron to the cooking pot, then take it out later?' We began thinking of adding a hunk of iron or iron ingots. I was working with a great group of people who were really motivated and well-connected."

Charles began communicating with iron ore smelting factories among Cambodia's larger manufacturing industries. The idea was to create an iron ore ingot that could be added to cooking pots. The first concept was an iron block about the size of a deck of cards. They were distributed to people in the area and Charles asked the women of the households to cook with them. It proved to be a challenge. There was resistance. But the Cambodian people knew Charles was a Canadian health care worker trying to help. He had started to gain their trust.

An even bigger challenge was the language and knowledge barrier. Most of the research subjects in the initial study had low levels of education, high rates of illiteracy, and a poor understanding of health in general.

"Anemia was an unknown concept," notes Charles. "They felt the way they felt — dizzy, tired, low energy. They didn't know that it might be related to their diets. I had some pretty rudimentary materials that I used, photos and basic PowerPoint graphics, to show 'This is how you feel today, this is the problem. And it's called anemia.' The way to treat it was to add more iron to their diets. It wasn't just a matter of handing out these iron blocks, but it was about getting people to understand why this is a problem that they should be concerned about and why I thought the iron block might be helpful."

It was the most sensible solution, it seemed, given how expensive iron pills were. Charles began to emphasize how using the iron blocks could benefit an entire family, noting anemic mothers give birth to underweight and anemic babies, continuing a harmful cycle that is difficult to break.

"That was a really important concept and an area that ultimately helped lead to the success of Lucky Iron Fish," Charles says.

He left the iron ingots in the communities for approximately three months then returned to interview the women and take blood samples to see if hemoglobin and iron levels had changed. That's when Charles experienced his first major research setback — a "complete and utter failure," as he describes it. The Cambodians had understood what he wanted them to do but it was such a foreign concept to add this piece of iron to their cooking pots. Charles gathered a collection of photos that showed what the people did think the iron was good for: propping up broken tables, using it as a doorstop or paperweight, among other uses.

"Kids were using them as toys, painting and drawing on them," Charles says. "Very few families were actually using them to cook. I heard from many people that the appearance was really quite discouraging. Cambodia is very much a food culture. A lot of your social life revolves around gathering as a group, gathering as a family, and eating food together, whether it's a plain bowl of rice or something special. People really do come together and value that ability to share a meal with one another.

"If you've got this ugly piece of iron and you're mixing that in with something that you've saved a lot of money to purchase … it's a struggle."

It was a massive learning experience for Charles. In addition to the poor visual appeal of the iron, he recognized that he had to do a better job explaining just how important it was to address anemia. He was frustrated that a few months of work was rendered essentially useless. Complicating matters was that he lived in a rural Cambodian house with no running water or electricity, but he somehow had to test blood samples. That hurdle required some ingenuity to overcome. When Charles first arrived in Cambodia, he attended an auction for equipment from a Russian-owned hospital that was closing down. He purchased a centrifuge that was approximately fifty years old and ran on car batteries. It wasn't possible to send the samples to the city to be tested, given the time it would take to get there, so Charles, Nary, and Tharith would run the tests at night at the house and try to make their own diagnoses.

Charles continued to communicate with the village elders and women in the study to address the concerns about the ingots and discuss what could be done to make the product more palatable, in addition to building on the education component. Charles found that the villagers thought the ingot would damage the cooking pot, and there was the issue of its lack of visual appeal. He focused on the latter point. He went through a couple of iterations of shapes, changing from a block with sharp corners to a simple disk. Then came a design that mimicked the lotus flower, a plant that is familiar to Cambodians, particularly in rice fields. The flower is also associated with good fortune, which seemed to be a good path to Charles.

Then on a walk through a marketplace, there was a light-bulb moment.

"I saw a gentleman whittling a piece of wood into a fish," said Charles. "Fish are absolutely the lifeblood of the Cambodian people. I thought, 'Well, that's an interesting idea.'"

Cambodia is mostly landlocked, with the Mekong River running through it. Communities rely heavily on fish, and it is the predominant protein source in the Cambodian diet. The wood carving was about the size of the ingot needed in the cooking pots. The fish was also an image seen everywhere in the country, a food source with which all Cambodians were familiar.

Charles took the idea and had a prototype made out of wood. It looked like a catfish and in focus groups it was a success. He remembers someone suggesting that the design should be based on a particular species of fish called try kantrop, which is considered lucky.

"It's a fish that they only eat when they're having a celebration," explains Charles. "One time a year perhaps, people get together and have it."

Charles now had the right shape and size, a good weight, and a flat design that maximized surface area, all while resembling a species of fish that the people cherished. It was a better product. About 150 were produced with the intent of repeating the initial study.

The next challenge for Charles was to address the anthropological aspect and see if he could change the behaviour related to using the fish. He sat down with the families in the study and started from square one, requesting that they use it for three months. Charles made sure to break down the information better. He explained that iron was a micronutrient and pointed out what could happen to people when they don't get enough of it and how that would impact the whole family.

"When I first moved to Cambodia, I began working with an NGO called Resource Development International — Cambodia, an organization that does a lot of work in water and sanitation, but they also had a small village health program," he explains. That's how he teamed up with the pair of individuals we introduced earlier, Nary, a pharmacist, and Tharith, a medical student who would go to school on the weekends.

That meant Tharith was available during weekdays, so the bulk of their work was conducted then and he would travel to Phnom Penh to study on weekends, which he did for five years.

"As I mentioned, both of them spoke only rudimentary English when we started working together and I spoke no Cambodian. But after I arrived in Cambodia, it wouldn't have been more than five or six days before the three of us moved into this hot, tiny village, Preak Russei."

Charles said that moving to the village was a culture shock for Nary and Tharith.

"They were doing village health work, but they weren't living in the villages that they were working in," he says. "They would go out for day trips and they would try to do small health interventions. They would help with building wells and things like that in communities that were funded by this NGO. But this was an experience, I think, for them to see what a different level of poverty looked like."

Charles benefitted from the fact the pair were health practitioners, but they had never done any research projects at this level before. It meant Charles had to engage in a certain amount of education, such as explaining how they were going approach the project, or how they would actually assess whether the iron fish was going to be effective or not. Another issue was how to build trust in the community.

"I had to learn a ton from them," Charles notes, pointing to the frustration and debilitating effects of the initial failed test. "I would say it was very much a collaboration to try to figure out how can we make this a successful project. I was incredibly intimidated. When they suggested that the first thing we had to do was to sit down with the village elders, I had no idea what that type of a meeting would even look like, or how to go about requesting it or what the proper protocol was, and how do you demonstrate respect to these elders in a way that is authentic."

The team of three had to figure out how to make the points that they needed to get across to folks who maybe didn't even understand the reasons they were there.

"That initial meeting was very challenging, and I remember being very worried about how that would go," Charles recalls. "Thankfully, in the end, it went very well. It was a bit of a dance, and they didn't know what to make of me and I didn't know what to make of them. You have to be willing in those circumstances to just put in the time and to make yourself a little humble and accept the fact that you're not going to be the one leading the charge."

The primary goal was to work with the community at large rather than singling out individuals. In the village in this case, there were an estimated eighty to ninety households and each would consist of roughly five to ten people. The goal was to work with the full community, with a focus primarily on impacting women's health.

"The first people that we had to reach out to were village elders, to get their buy-in, and specifically focusing on those village elders who were women themselves, who could help to sway the others to try to encourage them to look at this as something that's really important, not just for women, but for whole families," Charles explains. "That involved sitting down, having tea and spending hours in some cases, just talking through who we were, what we were there to do, what they could expect during our time in the village.

"We knew that we were not going to be able to work with all of the households in the village, we knew that there wouldn't be buy-in from all of them. But the idea was to essentially get a critical mass where there's enough people who are engaged in this, there's enough people who kind of understand and have the ability and time to cook meals on their own and to start using the iron fish. And we knew that word would spread to others. And so, as we continued, we would constantly get women coming to us and say, 'I am not part of your study, but I really want an iron fish. I go over to my neighbour, and I see it, I see how they're cooking with it. And I think I can do the same thing. How can I get one?'"

One of the challenges of any research study is that a stepwise approach is required to build that evidence base, to work with the community and see if over time the solution, the iron implement in this case, is going to be effective.

"Then at the end of that time, if we were successful, if the evidence was positive, and we showed that we could have an impact, we wanted to make sure that the iron fish was available to anyone else in the village who wasn't a part of the study," Charles says. "I think that built a lot of goodwill in that community. And I have no doubt that that goodwill spread, people talked about us. It was amazing, because we would go to neighbouring villages, on the way back to the NGO where we were now based, which was about a half-day trip, including two different ferries, and you're driving through a number of different villages and people come and say, 'Oh, you're the iron fish people. Come to our village because we want to be part of this, too.' And that was something that was really amazing. You could see that even before the research study had finished."

The word was spreading that this was a basic tool that was effective and easy to use.

"We weren't seeking people out and trying to twist their arms to be involved. They were reaching out to us," Charles says.

Success would require gaining a high enough level of trust from people who had been burned, despite good intentions, in the past. In the late 1980s and early 1990s, UNICEF initiated a program to get Cambodian villagers to change their drinking water habits because their current ones were making them sick. At the time, people were drinking from the river, where animals were bathed, where people bathed. The water was a muddy brown colour and teeming with bacteria. UNICEF went around to those communities and in each drilled two wells down into the groundwater and the communities changed their source of drinking water. What wasn't known at the time was that those two wells contained incredibly toxic levels of arsenic.

"They were telling communities that this was a safe source of drinking water, and they got the entire community on board," Charles says. "Then years later people started falling ill with arsenicosis, or arsenic poisoning. Folks would have cancers or really awful skin conditions, toughening and blistering of the hands and the feet. So it was very clear, especially to those who were a little bit older and had been drinking that water for longer, that they were really suffering from this and dying. As a result, there was a lot of lingering distrust about working with NGOs and folks from the outside. We were battling against that distrust."

Ultimately, UNICEF returned and capped the wells. Some of the work of the NGO that Charles had partnered with involved bringing water filters into the community. The ceramic water filters required no movable parts and villagers could use them to purify the river water.

"And then in addition to trying to regain trust, blood is seen as something that's sacred, as something that you don't spill," Charles says. "It's seen as part of their essence. So even though we were using it right there in the moment, running our lab tests, it had people worried, wondering what we were doing with that blood.

"We were outsiders, and Nary and Tharith were outsiders just as I was, even though they're Cambodian, because they weren't from that area. They were educated. It was apparent to people that they had more money, and we drove a car into this village that didn't have any cars. There was a lot of hesitation around that. It surprised me that it would be such a hurdle to get over and how important it was to demonstrate to people that this is something that's safe."

In that village and surrounding communities there were no doctors, and the nearest hospital was many kilometres away. As a result, villagers could not access the hospital, so they were not familiar with having blood taken.

"There is a lot of research looking at iron deficiency and income generation," says Charles. "We know that families that are iron deficient generate less income. The children do poorer in school. And there are greater rates of maternal anemia and hemorrhage in childbirth. The research shows why it's important to tackle the issue." Those conditions would eventually serve as a motivator for villagers once they recognized and identified the problem.

After developing trust and gaining the willingness of people to have their blood taken, the team still always had to get villagers to use the fish regularly. Charles and his partners had a strategy. They targeted some of the households where the "social butterflies" of the community lived. People would come to see the foreigners and groups would gather for cooking demonstrations. Nary, whom Charles describes as a "fantastic cook," showed how the fish was used. She would discuss recipes and how the iron fish could help. There is research showing that the acidity level of food is important in helping the iron to be absorbed. Using lemon when boiling water with the iron fish helps add acidity.

The team also returned on a monthly basis for blood samples and to remind the Cambodians in the study that they had not gone anywhere. Charles emphasized that they were there to answer questions and help in any way needed. This new plan proved to be much more effective.

"At the end of that three-month study, we were able to show that about ninety-five percent of our participants were still using the fish on a daily basis," says Charles. "That was a tremendous success given the disappointing outcomes with the iron ingots previously."

Charles and the team were certainly on the right track. But concerns remained. They wanted the products to be as pure as possible and it was difficult to get consistent, high-quality sources of iron. An underlying principle of the work was to "do no harm" and that thought was always front of mind for Charles. They worked very hard to source pure iron and, after about six attempts, found one source they were certain was good quality and free of contaminants.

The next step was to increase the scale of the project from both a production and a scientific perspective. In Canada, a test for anemia would assess about five to ten different lab values. When the team ran samples on the old centrifuge, they looked at one single lab value, hematocrit levels, which reveal how much of the blood is made up of red blood cells. More information was needed. Charles was confident in the results of the pilot study, but he knew he needed to be able to replicate the findings in a larger study, with potentially four to five hundred people. For the next year and a half, Charles focused on producing a bigger, more formalized, randomized control trial, tackling the logistics of increasing the scale.

The team had already expanded to six, a few new members having been added to help with the community relations aspect of the work. But getting around and transporting blood to labs was still a hurdle. Motos, or small motorcycles, are the main method of transportation in Cambodia, a hot country with limited refrigeration facilities which meant blood samples had to be sent quickly for testing rather than stored. The team began using a crew of moto drivers, who would strap the blood samples on their backs and deliver them to labs a few hours away. Around 6:00 a.m. the team would collect blood samples for the first half of the day before sending them off with the moto drivers.

Charles expanded the study population and fine-tuned the educational materials so that as he introduced the iron fish to different communities, everything was done the same way. Everyone had to be on the same page regarding how the messages were delivered. Trust, as always, was essential.

"One of the scourges of international development in Cambodia is that it's a country that suffered a great genocide and has had tremendous sadness in its political history," says Charles. "After the genocide, there was a large number of NGOs that went into Cambodia to try to help rebuild, I think almost as a penance for not having done more during the genocide itself. It led to a significant NGO presence, with some less than rigorous work being done.

"Very early on, I realized that if I was going to be successful in this work, I needed to think past my lab-bench mentality. I couldn't just be a scientist."

Charles embraced the idea that he needed to build an understanding of anthropology and culture and how to effectively communicate. His master's in biomedical science quickly transformed into a much more interdisciplinary project that required different levels of expertise.

More time passed for Charles in Cambodia. His initial three months turned into a year, then two. Ultimately, he would spend close to seven years with the people who had grown close to his heart. In about the second year of the journey, the Cambodian government saw value in the work, and a partnership was formed. Samples could now be tested at a lab in the capital city of Phnom Penh. Then it was time for a randomized control trial where one group used the iron fish, and one group didn't. The goal was to compare the health outcomes over time. Charles also developed a questionnaire that addressed quality of life outcomes, energy levels, headaches, and dizziness, and looked at signs and symptoms of anemia. He had come quite a long way since measuring a single lab value back in the old centrifuge days.

Also in that second year, a North American team was assembled, with people in British Columbia, Guelph, and the United States. By years three and four of the project, an anthropologist, an epidemiologist, a nutritionist, and a biomedical scientist joined in the interdisciplinary work. Charles's master's eventually turned into a Ph.D., which he completed at Guelph.

Throughout his years in Cambodia, Charles faced an internal struggle. He did not have a formal medical background but because he was discussing health and nutrition with the local people, many assumed he was a doctor. It was true he had a great amount of health knowledge, but there were challenges working in the communities.

"Someone brought their grandfather, who had had a machete accident, to see me," recalls Charles. "He had part of his foot chopped off. Or someone who had a stroke. I was constantly encountering these situations where people were asking me for help. I didn't have that medical training. I felt like I was asking so much of them, but I wasn't able to give them all that they needed in return. I became a bit of a self-taught, self-trained first responder. I was able to provide some help to these folks. But I wanted to make sure that if I was going to do this for the rest of my life, that I would have that high-quality skill set so that I could help as much as I possibly could.

"It was a privilege to be able to develop relationships with people who had such different lives from my own. I spent a lot of time in two particular communities where I lived. I started to develop a bit of a routine. I would encounter people every day and we would share stories. That was really positive from a personal perspective because sometimes I was just on my own. You need those human connections, while also trying to maintain that scientific approach and not wanting to influence things too much."

It was painful for Charles to see the poverty and lack of privilege compared to what he was fortunate to have. The Cambodians frequently suffered serious injuries or got infections, and in their environment, that could mean a death sentence. Those thoughts weighed heavily on him.

"It was really challenging to see what they were encountering day in, day out," he says. "I was rightfully focused on one area, anemia and nutrition, but it was at the expense of having to look past all of the other struggles I could see. That was tough."

The emotional toll aside, the work ultimately went well. His studies showed the iron fish worked and a great solution had been discovered. It made sense culturally, anthropologically, and scientifically. The next phase would be to scale it up, working in different areas of Cambodia, and other countries as well.

Personally, Charles had not intended to do a Ph.D., but his time in Cambodia took him down that path. He still had medicine in the back of his mind, too. He spent months considering whether to pursue more training in medicine or work on commercializing the iron fish.

"My interest from day one in this project was working with the people on the ground, getting to share stories, and see the impact of the work," explains Charles. "I had less interest in sitting in boardrooms, developing budgets, research proposals, and business plans. At that point, I considered bringing on someone who had more business experience to develop the next phase of the project.

"That allowed me to take a look and say, 'Now is the time to pursue additional training in medicine so that I can fulfill that skill set I thought was missing.'"

Charles had an incredible passion for the Lucky Iron Fish project. He wanted to see it move forward and be in good hands, with a team-based approach. He put out a call for applications. He knew a manufacturing acumen would be key, as would opting for the social business venture route, as opposed to working with NGOs.

"I think after we'd collected all this evidence to show that the iron fish could have great results, people were willing to use it, it was effective," Charles explains. "From an anecdotal perspective, people identified that their symptoms of anemia had gone away."

The team had demonstrated that the fish could be produced on a small scale and distributed.

"Step one, you have a successful public health intervention, then the next step is scaling up, and scaling up is a huge logistical challenge," he explains. "You need to find a manufacturer; you need to figure out how to get things from point A to point B. And you need to figure out how to market and how to keep your budget balanced when it's no longer a research project. And then if this is something that's going to continue in perpetuity, how are you actually going to make it work?"

It was those challenges that took Charles's thinking away from the public health side of things and much more into the business side, which he didn't see as his personal forte. And, all the while, a career in medicine continued to be on his mind.

"I grew up, I think as many doctors do, thinking that I wanted to be a doctor without really understanding what that meant," Charles says. "I don't come from a family of doctors at all and I'm the first in my family to work in health care. So I didn't really have much exposure, but it was always something that I wanted to do. I always really liked science and math and I liked helping people. So medicine seemed like the obvious path."

His undergraduate degree and then graduate school had reinforced a great interest in research. At the same time, reinforced by his experience working in Cambodian villages, he believed he was lacking a skill set. "That was the medicine background," he says. "There were many instances when I was following up with women who had an iron fish to take a blood sample or to talk to them about their usage, and they would start talking to me about their relative who was sick. They would ask if there was anything that we could do to help them. Or they would say their baby's not eating, or that they cut themselves really badly and it doesn't look good. And now there's pus seeping from the wound."

Charles points to one of the most striking examples that led to his interest in medicine. He went into a household to visit a woman, and he could hear a baby screaming.

"It was coming from the backyard," he recalls. "In villages there are lots of babies, but in this instance, we discovered a mother in great distress and were unsure what to do. In Cambodia, people in rural areas cook over an open fire, and her toddler — I imagine about two years old — had fallen into the fire and burned both hands quite badly. They had no idea what to do, and I'm talking fingers down to stubs and a very, very bad burn.

"They had gone to the local health centre, which was staffed by folks that you would hope were doctors and nurses but are often not that. They're often someone with a little bit of extra training who can maybe give out bandages and things of that nature.

"In this case the child's hands were wrapped up and they were sent home after being told there was nothing else that they could do. We arrived a couple of days after the accident had occurred, and the mother was overwhelmed and distraught because obviously something bad had happened. And she doesn't know how to access health care for her baby. She can't afford it. She can't get onto the back of a moto and drive to Phnom Penh and go to a children's hospital.

"So we see this baby and she's got these horrific wounds and filthy bandages," Charles says. "You can just see this is not going to go well. And in instances like that, as a researcher in public health, you can't go in and have an agenda. You don't want to speak to the woman about how she's using the iron fish. Even as a non-physician, you know that you need clean bandages, and you need to keep the wounds clean. There are basics that need to happen."

In the end Charles says he always felt that if he were to have an impact on global health, "I had to have that background of medicine in order to be able to help the folks that I'd encounter along the way. So it was a combination of those things. One, sort of that childhood dream of being a doctor, and then, that realization in the moment as you're working, doing this research, that okay, both of these things would be useful and helpful to have together."

He points to his sense of helplessness and being overwhelmed by the heat, smells, and noise. Charles describes it as sensory overload, coupled with witnessing what true poverty looks like.

"It's overwhelming," he says, "yet you're pulled in different directions. You're trying to focus on the iron fish as well, but I couldn't at the same time turn a blind eye to suffering."

In the case of the burned little girl, Charles and his colleagues dropped what they were doing and took the child and her mom in the backseat of the car and drove them to the children's hospital. Then through the help of the NGO and other donors they scraped together enough money to pay for her care.

"You can't turn a blind eye to something like that, right?" he says. "You'd never be able to sleep; it would be something that would haunt you. Sure, you've got an agenda. You want to try to impact people's nutrition, but you can't do that in a vacuum. You have to take into account the other things that person or that family is experiencing at that time."

Charles said he and his partners didn't see the child again but were told she stayed in the children's hospital in Phnom Penh for several weeks where they gave regular dressing changes, pain medication, and extended help for the little girl.

"It's sad, though, because I know that that kid likely ended up back in a household that was very, very poor," he adds, noting the unlikelihood that her family could escape that poverty any time soon.

The gut-wrenching experiences, the persistent drive toward medicine to try to make a difference, and the recognition that he had a limited skill set when it came to the business side of Lucky Iron Fish were all conspiring to point Charles on a new course.

"I think one thing that we often see from international development is we have really great content experts, people who are experts in public health, people who are experts in nutrition, or water and sanitation," he says. "But we don't often engage with private industry and with folks who are great at business and all of those logistics to make large-scale intervention successful. I do think there's a value in bringing in people that have specific skill sets that aren't your own.

"I think that there was an interest level for me in whether this could be effective and whether we could change people's lives. But when it came to the next steps, I saw that as something that was going to pull me away from the engagement that I was able to have with folks living in villages, and instead having to take a step back, work more remotely, manage budgets and supply chains and things of that nature. It was a very, very difficult challenge."

Charles recognized what his interests and limitations were and wondered if there could be someone who could have an impact.

"The goal was always to have the biggest impact that we could possibly have and show that this was going to be useful," he says. "We wanted to make sure that we could help as many people as possible to have a fish in their home. I felt that the goal was going to be more quickly achieved by someone, or a team of people, who had a different skill set than what I had."

The time had come to try to find an individual or team that could grow that dream. Among the proposals, one applicant seemed to stand out. Gavin Armstrong displayed the characteristics being sought — a business education background and an interest in global health and social justice.

"It was rare," notes Charles. "You often see people who are either business or development inclined, but to bridge those two worlds was harder to find." Armstrong had that unique ability, and the stage was set for the next phase in the evolution of Lucky Iron Fish.

"Gavin connected with Chris when he was in university," Linda Armstrong, Gavin's mother, recalls. "As I understand it, Chris had other interests and that is how Gavin became involved with Lucky Iron Fish. He started with just doing a thesis based on work in Cambodia, and as he was working on getting his Ph.D., he recognized the concept could be developed as a business. I was so happy that Gavin went this way. He was thinking of working at a bank or whatever; he wanted to be rich. But he went a different way."

In the meantime, Charles went on to complete medical school at McMaster University in Hamilton, Ontario. Today he remains a part of the Lucky Iron Fish board. His analytical nature and genuine love of research were critical to the project's success, especially after those early, dark moments of failure when Charles still chose to persevere.

"The story of the Lucky Iron Fish is that after that initial three-month study, I could have looked at it and said, 'Ah, no one is interested in putting these iron ingots in their cooking pots. Let's move on.'

"But I forced myself to look at what worked and what didn't. I tried to be humble and lay it out to those around me. Having that collaborative approach is one of the most important aspects of overcoming failures."

# Chapter 3

# Gavin Armstrong and His Challenging Youth

WITH THE SUCCESS of the critical research by Christopher Charles in Cambodia in place, the transition toward developing a business model began. Charles had identified Gavin Armstrong as having a unique combination of experience, skills, and interests, so it's valuable to examine the path the new leader followed to arrive at such a point in his career. That examination will come from Armstrong himself, his friends, and his family, starting with his father.

John Armstrong admires many of his son's qualities. Gavin is unwilling to accept failure. He is also principled, fearless, and honest to his very core, John says. These characteristics have provided a solid foundation in both his personal and professional life and have been instrumental in the growth of Lucky Iron Fish.

But that resilience and unwillingness to break were forged out of necessity. Armstrong suffered terribly throughout his childhood and adolescence, having to deal with one battle after the next. He was mercilessly bullied at school. Years of abuse took an incredible toll to the point where Armstrong harmed himself. Thoughts of suicide manifested into actual attempts to take his own life. The memories are painful, but the strength within Armstrong allowed him to overcome these experiences.

Gavin Armstrong was born in January 1987. He made his first appearance two weeks past his due date.

Once Gavin did show up, he attacked everything with energy. By nine months of age, he was already up and running, perhaps foreshadowing the mobility and incredible journeys to come throughout his life. He has travelled the world, but Gavin spent most of his early days in Kilbride, Ontario, a small town just northwest of Burlington. His parents, John and Linda, grew up in Streetsville, in the heart of Mississauga. The couple wanted something different for their young son and a new child on the way. Linda was pregnant with Gavin's sister, Shannon, when they left Streetsville and moved to Kilbride.

"We decided we were going to take root in Kilbride," says John, a retired high-school science teacher. "Gavin was already with us and Shannon was born there. We thought the place was ideal — a one-church, one-general-store, one-school kind of a town. But when you get into a little town like that, there is not a lot of diversity. In this little hamlet, you had millionaire mansions and farms, a real disparity."

There were also expectations placed on the community's members. For example, boys in Kilbride were expected to play baseball. That proved difficult for Gavin. He was thin, lacking competitive fire, and was not necessarily interested in sports. He also had terrible allergies. These attributes made him a target, and the kids in Kilbride were unrelenting, making life hard for the newcomer.

"I was bullied for as long as I can remember," recalls Armstrong. "It began in elementary school. They called me stupid nicknames, like 'Gayvin.' It took me many years to realize I was gay, but at seven years old, I didn't. I always felt that I didn't fit in, and acting effeminate put a target on my back.

"I would get beat up and teased, both verbal and physical abuse. It followed me into high school. I tried to attend a different high school than everyone else in my age group but on my first day, there was freshman hazing, and they wrote *faggot* on my forehead in permanent marker. I had been hoping to start from scratch. It didn't go well.

"They were dark times. I have started talking about them more at public engagements. Students come up to me and say that it's really important to hear what happened to me and encouraging to know that there is a light at the end of the tunnel."

Armstrong says he always felt like a loner. He and Shannon would stay at a local caregiver's while their parents worked. The other children played with Shannon, but he remembers being more of an outsider himself. He would spend that time climbing trees or just imagining things, like being in the movie *Star Wars*. That isolation continued at school. Armstrong says he particularly hated the lunch hour because of the option to sit anywhere you wanted.

"I always had to sit by myself," he says. "You stand out because you're alone."

Linda has vivid memories of the bullying her son endured. He wanted to be actively involved in committees and school councils, and he was courageous enough to try, which was beneficial because it gave him his first experiences with public speaking. It did, however, cause stress.

"Gavin was so nervous about the taunting that his hands would start to shake," Linda says. "They wouldn't stop. As soon as he woke up in the morning, his hands would shake. That was in about grade four or five. Doctors couldn't find anything wrong with him and the kids would say that he was making it up.

"It was horrible. It was difficult as a parent to witness. I felt helpless trying to figure out how to resolve it."

Gavin eventually left public school late in grade eight, opting to be home-schooled for the last couple of months of the academic year. The daily abuse was too much to endure.

But throughout these childhood ordeals, there was an aspiring entrepreneur waiting to emerge. Gavin was adamant about getting a job at an early age. By the time he was twelve, he was working at the Kilbride general store. John thought he was too young for the work, and the bullying continued even while he was on the job. Kids spat on him and threw things directly at him or on the ground outside the store, knowing that Gavin would be tasked with the cleanup. He just put his head down and did the work.

By the age of sixteen, his desire to get into business was growing more sophisticated. Gavin started his own micro businesses, buying and selling things such as video games. Once he thought of an idea for a product he wanted to invent — an electronic lock for a locker, one that could be opened with a clicker like a car. At the age of sixteen Gavin was calling lawyers and getting quotes for patents. In the end the cost of pursuing the idea was too great for his monthly allowance to support.

"Gavin always recognized the power of technology," his father notes.

He certainly understood technology, but he was also motivated. Armstrong had a taste for business and wanted to pursue it as a career. A time would eventually come at the University of Guelph when he would find his true calling. Lucky Iron Fish provided a bridge between being a business-savvy decision-maker and meeting the needs of people around the world who required help, which ultimately meant much more to him than simply being a successful salesperson.

Conflict surrounded him. He could not avoid it. Armstrong's parents argued regularly, which imprinted heavily on him, something he has learned through therapy as an adult. Eventually John and Linda divorced.

"I experienced a lot of trauma as a kid, and that has impacted the way my brain thinks and reacts to things," he says. "My parents obviously cared a lot about me and saw the effect everything was having on me. They offered to let me change my name. They were prepared to offer support.

"I didn't have a good relationship with Shannon growing up. We were at odds all the time. We each had our favourite parent and that caused tension. We were jealous of each other, thinking the other was receiving more love. But when I came out, she was the first family member I told. She was very supportive, and since then, we have become quite close."

Gavin and John also struggled to have a strong relationship. John says it wasn't so much that he argued with his son, but more that there was a general unpleasant vibe and lack of co-operation between them. They simply weren't close.

"There was an awful lot of stress when he was growing up," recalls John. "Looking back, it's now easier to understand the con-flicts that existed. And conflict is the right word. When he was a teenager, I thought he hated me. We've talked about that and when I told him, he looked rather hurt. But we were on such different pages. He was struggling with his identity and not knowing it, and, of course, I had no clue. You proceed with the framework of your own ideals, the mechanisms which make you work. And then you realize his are in flux, and mine were carved in stone. We weren't meshing."

It wasn't for lack of effort. John tried to make it work at times. He was a Cubs co-leader in Kilbride and wanted Gavin involved in the group. But attempts like those didn't seem to pan out. John says he always loved his son and admired him, though they were admittedly frustrated with each other.

"My parents pushed me into things that probably caused me to be resistant," Gavin says. "They put me in soccer and T-ball, then two years of sea cadets, and jiu-jitsu. I had especially bad allergies in the summer. I'd wake up with my eyes swollen shut, and being outside was just uncomfortable. That's a stereotypical nerdy thing, that you can't play sports because of allergies, and you start to stand out. You're self-identifying as a loner. In a sense, you're pointing a finger at yourself."

Armstrong would therefore punish himself with constant attempts to self-harm. This evolved into more serious behaviours, as he began cutting himself frequently and even trying to find ways to end his life. He was once rushed to hospital after he had ingested chemicals from his father's science-class supplies. He began therapy around that time, both alone and with the family, though he remembers not always being sincere or honest in the sessions.

The self-destructive path continued and interactions with other children remained painful. Armstrong recounts one story that had a lasting impact. Some kids came by on bikes and asked him to play hide-and-seek. It seemed like a genuine opportunity, but it ended in heartbreak.

"They were just playing with me," says Armstrong. "I hid and they went back to their houses to play video games. I guess they were laughing at the thought of me hiding for hours."

Both Armstrong and his parents were paralyzed by this environment. John was angry about what was happening to his son at school and in the community, and that little was done to address the abuse. At Gavin's grade-eight graduation, one of the kids honoured was one of Gavin's bullies. He had once held him down on the school bus and tried to shove grass in his mouth.

"I was quite incensed," John remembers. "I almost walked out. I could not believe that they would pick the most overt bully and say he was the prize student."

John felt that the school mismanaged the situations Gavin faced. Before he left the classroom in those last months of grade eight, Gavin would come home and make it clear that he had gone through a tough day. John was at a tipping point. He wanted to address the issues with the school staff, but Gavin pleaded with his father not to, knowing there would be ramifications.

"I said, 'Enough is enough,'" John recalls. "As a teacher and a parent, I had to do what I felt was my duty. I went in and had an interview with Gavin's teacher. She was very understanding.

"A couple of days later, Gavin came home, looked down, and said, 'Thanks, Dad.' What happened was that he was in class and asked to go to the bathroom. While he was gone, the teacher told the students to stop bullying Gavin. How do you think that would go over with twelve- and thirteen-year-olds? I felt so bad for him. He told me that it was like walking into a room with a bunch of vicious dogs. That's the feeling he had when he stepped into the class. All eyes were on him. They wouldn't talk to him."

Despite the obvious roadblocks in school, Gavin excelled academically. His marks were solid and graduating on time was never in doubt. High school was the next challenge facing him and the family. John was a staunch supporter of the public school system. He remembers being initially disappointed when he learned that Gavin made the decision to attend Notre Dame, a Catholic school in Burlington.

Apparently, Linda gave John a very distinct "shut-up-and-listen" glare. John did just that, and it ended up being the right decision. Only a few of the Kilbride bullies went to the Catholic school and, ultimately, Gavin met a good group of kids. His parents welcomed them into their home regularly and were buoyed by the fact that their son was experiencing some actual joy socially.

Jennifer Souter was one of the people that Armstrong met at Notre Dame. Today, the Toronto-based counsellor works in the social services sector as a peer supporter for young people living with mental health challenges and addiction. Souter wasn't particularly close with Armstrong at Notre Dame, but they ran in parallel circles. They each went off to university and then reconnected in 2016 at a Pride event.

"I ran into him outside in the street and since then, we've built a friendship," says Souter, who like Armstrong is openly gay. "That encounter was impactful for me because I wasn't out in high school. I didn't know I was gay in high school. Gavin and I weren't very close then, so I didn't know that about him either. Running into him at Pride was a bit of an 'aha moment.' That commonality brought us back together."

While Armstrong experienced a generally more peaceful existence at Notre Dame than in Kilbride, it was still not ideal. There was the hazing on his first day when he was pushed into a corner and restrained while seniors wrote the derogatory word *faggot* on his forehead.

"I had to go back to class like that," Armstrong recalls. "I tried to rub it off. I think back to the teachers and them not really doing anything about it. At the same time, I didn't want to point the finger and get beat up for the rest of my life. That was day one."

He continued to have challenges through his first two years at Notre Dame. He was once beaten up at a school dance for "dancing too gay." Armstrong did love to swim and thought he would try out for the school team, which would be both a great activity and a way to make friends. As he entered the orientation, he saw that one of the kids who'd participated in the hide-and-seek prank was there.

"I just turned around and left," he says. "I had an anxiety attack seeing that person."

In grade ten, Armstrong went on a school field trip. Students wore uniforms at Notre Dame but for trips, they were allowed to wear everyday clothes. He wore a recently purchased baby blue turtleneck sweater that he really liked. But his classmates were relentless, asking if it was his mom's sweater and if he was a cross-dresser. Armstrong went to the bathroom and hid, letting the bus leave without him.

That night he attempted to take his own life again.

Eventually, Armstrong built stronger relationships, sometimes by any means necessary. The bus ride from Kilbride to Notre Dame was about half an hour, or put another way, thirty minutes of hell when there were bullies aboard. He remembers a brother and sister pair who lived near his house. He began to talk with them on the bus and at school. The siblings would go to a location known as the "smokers' pit" to light up cigarettes.

"I actually took up smoking so I could be there and away from the bullies," Armstrong says. "I hated smoking, but it was an excuse to get away. Thinking back, we were all outsiders in our own way."

Souter wasn't at all aware of the challenges that Armstrong faced back in high school, and they were only revealed as their friendship grew over recent years. She laments not knowing him better. They could have helped each other.

"I now know of the struggles he had," she says. "I'm not saying mine were the same, but I definitely have had my fair share. I wish I had known and that we were closer then. If two people are going through a shitty situation, they can at least go through it together. My friendship with him is a nice one to have. I rarely keep in contact with people from high school so it's nice to have somebody who was there for those things.

"I remember him being very shy," Souter adds. "The environment really bred that if you were in any way different. Our high school was not very quick at shutting that down. But Gavin surprises and impresses me. We were Facebook friends, and I would see things, like when he was running for student government in university. I had no idea that was something that interested him.

"You can see his progression. My wife and I watched his *Dragons' Den* episode recently and he's now in this place where he's so confident. It's honestly quite powerful to see."

That transformation began in Armstrong's last two years at Notre Dame. He found a different group of friends, individuals who stayed away from the vices he had taken up as a young high-school kid. Armstrong believes that it was around that time that he began to embrace his sexuality and exactly who he was.

"I felt more comfortable being with girls and being friends with girls," he says. "I found this group and they were friends with other guys. I became their 'plus one.' I always had that awkwardness, and I still don't think I fully get along with guys as much as girls. But I had a group of friends that I could go to class with and sit beside and have lunch with. I came into my own.

"I felt less vulnerable. You're not alone. You're walking down the hallway with three people, which is much different than sitting by yourself. I was still nervous in the main areas where everyone hung out. That's where you were a target. But I felt safer. I was on student government, and I took a victory lap, which meant doing another semester after grade twelve because I needed to get my English grade higher."

Most of the bullies had left Notre Dame by that point. He took English, did co-op, and even made up for his previously missed opportunity by joining the swim team.

"My best high-school period was that last semester," he recalls.

The healing Armstrong experienced as a teenager would be critical to the person he would become. And it shows in all the facets of his life. Staying in therapy has also been beneficial to his well-being. In recent years, he has participated in Eye Movement Desensitization and Reprocessing (EMDR) therapy, which helps those who have experienced trauma. The concept is that trauma literally leaves scar tissue on the brain and the result is a feeling of always being on alert and never safe. It's a psychological issue, and the therapy has made Armstrong more compassionate and, overall, less angry.

Armstrong also has a stronger relationship with his parents today. His mother, Linda, works alongside him as a Lucky Iron Fish administrator, handling things like payroll, expenses, and accounts receivable. Armstrong has also made progress with John. Since 2016, John has suffered from idiopathic pulmonary fibrosis (IPF), a serious chronic disease that affects the tissue surrounding the air sacs, or alveoli, in the lungs. This condition develops when that lung tissue becomes thick and stiff for unknown reasons. John had severe inflammation in his lungs and needed a lung transplant, which he had in 2020. The pandemic also had an impact on the health care system, making his challenges even greater.

The silver lining to that transplant ordeal is he and Gavin have shared more time together.

"Gavin has just been a rock," says John. "He really stood out a lot those few months. He visited me every day in the hospital. It's part of his growth, too, his development and the way he has progressed as an adult."

They have gotten closer as time has gone on. When John chats on the phone with Gavin, he is content to simply listen to what's happening in his son's unique and interesting life. It can't make up for the lost time, but it is special considering that for years they rarely spoke.

"I think that what goes around comes around. It took time for me to have an impact on him. I wasn't there when he was growing up. I wasn't there until he got into this [career]. I think we can be unaware of the impact our parents have on us. As we grow up, we have character issues and belief systems that might be hidden, and it takes the right circumstances to bring them out. And then suddenly, like an old memory, it comes out."

A painful childhood was influential in carving Gavin Armstrong's path. Despite his trauma, he developed those qualities his parents most admire — being principled, fearless, honest, and perhaps most telling, a survivor and refusing to quit.

By the time Armstrong was ready to attend the University of Guelph, he was more in tune with who he was as a person. Once there, he would learn how to put his many talents to better use. His world view was changing. And seeing strife in remote corners of the planet helped Armstrong find a direction that would positively impact thousands of lives.

# Chapter 4

# Personal Development at the University of Guelph

GAVIN ARMSTRONG ARRIVED at the University of Guelph in 2006. At the time, the skinny kid from Kilbride had a clear image in his mind of the career he desired and the man he wanted to become. The plan was to be a banker, to achieve great financial success and, in turn, throw it back in the faces of all those people who had bullied him throughout a trying childhood.

"I had put it in my head at some point in high school that money equals respect, worth, and self-value," he explains. "The clothes I wore, I didn't have money for them, but I would try to wear the best brand names because I wanted to be seen as valuable. Banking on Bay Street looked like it equalled success."

He played the part ... for a while. Armstrong started as a commerce student at U of G majoring in economics and finance before eventually switching majors to marketing and consumer studies in his third year. From a young age, he had shown an ability to broker deals and make things happen. The commerce and finance program provided a foundation for him to achieve the goal of attaining wealth, he felt. To hide his gay identity or increase his sense of worth, in the past he had even envisioned himself arriving at a high-school reunion years down the road, with a wife and expensive car in tow.

But Armstrong quickly realized that the academic program he had chosen wasn't for him. He hated the classes, which focused heavily on economics and financial theory. His grades suffered as a result. And socially, the university environment wasn't what he envisioned. Armstrong had gained more confidence in the years prior to Guelph, in particular in his final semester at Notre Dame, his Catholic high school in Burlington, where he blossomed. He finally found friends who had a positive impact on his life, excelled in classes, and he took part in various activities, like joining the swim team. It appeared as if the years of abuse from the people in Kilbride and his high-school bullies were finally behind him.

"I remember wanting to start fresh in university and be my authentic self," he recalls. "I was going to be gay and make new friends, maybe gay friends. On my first day of orientation, some people on the floor of my residence were hanging out in a room and making plans to go out that night. I wanted to be included. One of my floormates pulled me aside and said, 'Hey, I have an awkward question. You're not gay, are you?' I could tell from the tone he wasn't happy. I said, 'No, no I'm not.' He said that was good and that they were uncomfortable inviting me if I was.

"I jumped right back in the closet. That undid all of the confidence I had built up and I ended up staying in the closet for the first three years of university. I hung out with those guys on the floor, the homophobic people. I was friends with them for three years."

He initially struggled to adapt to this new world. He said he drank more than he should have to cope with his internal struggle and to numb the feelings of loneliness. But Armstrong did find the odd ray of light. He enrolled in a first-year seminar course titled Politics, Science and the Environment. It was problem-based learning and he loved it. The fascinating part to him was that students were presented with a problem, and each of them was assigned a topic to research. They would assemble and teach each other what they had learned. At the end of each class, the students were tasked with giving feedback to each other and, ultimately, receiving feedback for themselves. The consensus was that Armstrong was too quiet and not tuned in enough.

"It was because I felt out of place and didn't feel as smart as everyone else, or felt I was incompetent," he says. "It was a major lack of confidence.

"Then in one of the classes, the problem involved something with business. I said that I would research that part. I was always so fascinated and intrigued with business. I came back and gave a great presentation. People were asking me questions and I was answering appropriately. In that particular group process, everyone said it was like night and day, and that I was a different person. It was those people that I felt inferior to making that observation about me.

"I finally found my footing in the group. I began to participate equally and became engaged. I was in the closet at this point, trying to understand my sexuality. I wanted to come out, but I was struggling, hiding, and wearing that mask, which probably impacted my feeling of inferiority and lack of confidence."

The course was run by Dr. Alastair Summerlee, introduced in Chapter 2, who was the University of Guelph president at the time Armstrong took the course. Working with Summerlee began to change Armstrong's perspective and world view. The class opened the door to international travel, and once he saw what was happening outside of the small town where he had lived, the aspiring banker began to value things differently. Maybe craving wealth and showing off to the bullies was a selfish thought. His talents could be used in much more productive ways.

One of Armstrong's first instructors at the university was Melanie Lang. Lang, who owns her own firm, Melanie Lang

Consulting, was also the academic adviser for the marketing program when he was there. Because Armstrong was becoming interested in courses outside of the Bachelor of Commerce core requirements, Lang worked with him to try to figure out how he could receive credit for some experiential learning opportunities. "At the time, experience education was alive and well," she says. "We were required to be creative thinkers. I saw that Gavin's interest in community aligned with my own, so there was a natural affinity to work together.

"Gavin and I were both interested in trying to figure out how you could take the theory and learning from your required courses and apply it in settings where you would be able to have an impact and demonstrate a social return on investment. The investment was your time and knowledge. It was really exciting to see a student who was very passionate about community and making a difference, using his knowledge to do so. Even before Lucky Iron Fish, he had a very evident concern for community and being involved."

Armstrong immersed himself in independent studies and travelled to low- to middle-income countries, working in rural communities. He wanted to address access to amenities and other things that we often take for granted in first-world societies. Armstrong sought Lang's advice and ran ideas by her, focusing on details like organizational structure and planning.

"He was always on his own entrepreneurial journey," she says. "He was an entrepreneurial student, an entrepreneurial researcher, and he was entrepreneurial in terms of being a business development person. He has grown and evolved over the years. His passion, skill set, energy, and drive were always applied to wherever he was and whatever he was working on."

Armstrong's first trip outside North America was to Oxford University in the United Kingdom. In 2007, a group of students from Guelph was invited to participate in mock trade negotiations, mimicking the Doha Round conducted by the World Trade Organization. Armstrong was excited to take part and intrigued with the global business theme. By the time the students returned, Summerlee had received an email from an individual involved in the mock negotiations saying how impressive the group was. The group worked so well that when the semester ended Summerlee felt compelled to keep them together, so they all participated in a field course over the summer to "keep the learning going."

The group's field course took them to Botswana for ten days. It was an eye-opening experience for Armstrong and influential in his career path. Those ten days changed his life, he is convinced. The central focus for the group was ecotourism, and specifically, creating a community-based tourism initiative. It was critical for the students to understand what the Botswana people were looking for and what opportunities existed.

Armstrong admits that he was "completely outside of my comfort zone." They camped in the southern African bush, and he felt foolish sporting his brand-new cargo shorts and backpack. He stayed quiet for much of the trip and became increasingly aware of his privilege. Armstrong is unsure if the itinerary was intentional, but at the beginning, the sights were spectacular. He saw the majesty of Victoria Falls, and then in Botswana he stayed in game reserves in the mountains, eating unique food and seeing beautiful animals.

But he saw more in the background, such as the horrible conditions behind the tourism, the poor pay for employees, the lines of people seeking health care, and the struggling schools. Armstrong saw inequality, and after one particular visit to a local slum, he was troubled knowing that he could drive back to have a nice dinner, while reminiscing about the day. The slum had shacks maybe fifty square feet in size, with many people crammed inside. There was no running water, limited electricity, and garbage strewn all over the ground. The children were thin and looked malnourished, with distended bellies, making Armstrong recall the commercials he'd seen on television while growing up that asked for money to support starving kids.

"My mom would change the channel because it upset her," Armstrong says. "But when you're there, you can't change the channel. It's in your face. You actually have to look and acknowledge it. You don't get to close your eyes and pretend it doesn't exist."

He went home having made a pledge to himself.

"Botswana was different than any country I had been to before," Armstrong recalls. "It was an incredible trip filled with wildlife and people and culture. But it was my first time seeing abject poverty and malnutrition up close. When I came back and reflected on that trip, I realized that I was on a very selfish trajectory to make money and prove the bullies wrong, people who I was never going to see again.

"That's when I decided I should be focusing on what my passions were and trying to solve these problems. I knew business could have a role in it. I shifted my major from finance to marketing, with a focus on corporate social responsibility. In my volunteerism, I became much more engaged in hunger-related issues."

Dr. Nathan Lachowsky met Armstrong when they were both students in the first-year seminar back in 2007. Now a professor at the University of Victoria's School of Public Health & Social Policy, he recalled that Armstrong was unlike any other business student in that he participated in these interdisciplinary studies, which shaped thought and focus.

"It changed all of us in how we viewed the world," says Lachowsky. "It created frustration around complacency, and the drive to really do something different to create an impact. It was born out of that interdisciplinary perspective or that political exposure of what is the role of science, business, and society and how all of those things come together to impact people's well-being."

Lachowsky was paired with Armstrong for the Botswana trip. He had been to the country before and was inspired to go back. The two became friends. Lachowsky was impressed by many things about this travel mate, including Armstrong's creativity around seeking solutions that didn't yet exist and bringing them to life.

"Gavin was incredibly friendly on these journeys," adds Lachowsky. "He loved being in new places and talking to people. If there was an activity to be done, he was the first to put his hand up to volunteer. He tried hard, he was gregarious and fun. He is one of those people who creates ease around him by being approachable, accessible, and an interested person. It engenders good relations with the people you encounter. It's very humanizing and honest."

Significant change was happening in Armstrong's life, and a personal decision made all the difference. After Botswana, he came out of the closet. Years of denying who he was had exhausted him. When the weight of Armstrong's sexual identity was off his shoulders, he said it felt like he could fly. "It was like a new me."

He told his sister first. Then on Easter Monday in 2010, Armstrong revealed what he had been hiding to his father.

"Gavin told me that he was queer," John recalls. "I didn't understand what he was saying, and that maybe it was a phase he was going through. It took me a long time to understand it.

"I had some friends at work who were gay, and one was a woman guidance counsellor. I told her, 'I've got to talk with you because my son is gay.' I said that it must have been a choice he made, and she went off the rails. I thought she was going to take my head off. She said, 'Why would anyone choose this?' She went on to explain that you don't choose it. That's why there is stigma and discrimination. The misunderstanding is that people equate it to lifestyle and therefore, it's a choice. That isn't right. Gavin chose to step out. The struggles he had with bullying helped him realize his own identity. He does not understand the meaning of failure. It's not part of his vocabulary."

This marked a major shift in Armstrong's life. He was energized and he began to work at a furious pace. He ran for student government and won. He was elected as the Communications and Corporate Affairs Commissioner for the U of G student union. He served on the university's senate, the board of governors, and the president's task force on sustainability. Armstrong was on the steering committee and cabinet for the BetterPlanet Project, the university's major fundraising campaign, while also acting as student co-chair for the annual United Way Campaign. In 2012, he was working toward a master's in rural planning and development but then he was fast-tracked into a Ph.D. in biomedical science with a focus in iron deficiency and studying the efficacy of the Lucky Iron Fish, which at that time was called Happy Fish. He completed his Ph.D. in 2016.

"Gavin is one of the most tenacious people I know," says Dr. Kyly Whitfield, an associate professor at Mount Saint Vincent University and a close friend of Armstrong's dating back to their undergrad days in Guelph. "He is always busy. If he's not organizing something, he's reading the news ferociously."

The concept of "social business" didn't really exist when Armstrong was a student in Guelph. Then he took a class that focused on corporate social responsibility, which proved very interesting. It prompted Armstrong to co-found a club named Net Impact, where members promoted sustainable business practices on campus.

"It was very Guelph," he explains. "We were trying to make significant institutional changes with five students, but we were supported by the university."

At Guelph, Armstrong found himself in an environment that was aligned with his concerns about social responsibility, borne out by the fact that the school was named world's most caring university. That reputation was built from a way of thinking that can be traced right back to the university's roots.

"I would say it goes back to the original founding colleges, with veterinary, the agricultural college, and I guess, as they called it at the time, home economics," explains Jason Moreton, vice-president, external, at Guelph. "These really did help develop the ethos of the university, when it comes to that caring instinct. When you think about it, the whole farm-to-the-plate idea was really important and the whole community is involved in looking out for one another. Those things seem to be built in the foundation."

Moreton points to Armstrong's initial exposure to the culture at Guelph and how it inspired his evolution.

"He had an opportunity that I think differentiates University of Guelph from others, for he was someone who had the attention of senior administration and was able to get support from a wide array of faculty," Moreton says. He points to the first-year seminar Armstrong took with Summerlee as an example. At the time, the young student was shy and had fragile confidence, so Summerlee gave him a challenging task.

"If I remember correctly, the task was about trying to get in front of somebody at a bank," Moreton explains. "Gavin was given so much encouragement that he was able to track down this person by waiting outside in the hallway of the bank in order to get a meeting that Alastair [Summerlee, as university president] himself couldn't get. The opportunity for him to have that backing from faculty and the president of the university was really instrumental."

At the time, the university was planning for a capital fundraising campaign which, not surprisingly, became the BetterPlanet Project.

"So you know, as we're going through that campaign we had the student experience at the heart of any conversation we had externally," Moreton says.

The development of Lucky Iron Fish was taking place and the idea of taking such a concept to solve a major problem "was a proof point for us with the BetterPlanet Project. We actually had students who had an idea, and we were able to take that idea and start to use it for our own fundraising purposes."

When the three founding colleges were united to form the University of Guelph in 1964, it would have been understandable if some of those cultural traits, the caring community Moreton described earlier, had been lost, but they survived the transition.

"It seems that was built into the fabric, too," Moreton says, adding that today the school's "differentiator when students are on campus for a campus visit is that they are actually seen as people and welcomed as a part of the school. I still recall students talking about how crazy it is that people at the University of Guelph hold the door open for other people."

Moreton points to Bill Winegard, who served as Guelph's second president from 1967 to 1975, for reinforcing that image of the school.

"He would say you don't know where you're going if you forget where you've been," Moreton recalls. "That's one of the things that we'll continue to talk about, an issue that feels right at the university, that nobody succeeds if somebody falls behind.

"I think during Gavin's time, and obviously, when he was a student, and still true today, that there's a huge amount of student support. This experience seems relevant to me. The other day I saw somebody on the phone, a student, and she was crying, and she was all by herself. And as I was walking by and could see that she was crying, three strangers gathered to see if she was okay."

Moreton says that as new university presidents arrived at Guelph over the years, they were "almost compelled to accept that this is the culture that they have inherited here."

In the area of fundraising, such as in the naming of the business school, the theme the school wanted to project was sustainable business as a force for good, which was one of the traits that attracted benefactor Stu Lang and family.

"They didn't want to have a regular business school," Moreton said. "They wanted one that cared about how to leave communities stronger and more sustainable rather than just bottom-line dollars. That was part of our roots, the culture, so that was relevant to Stu when he was getting involved with the business school."

That way of thinking continues to resonate with Lang. Moreton says that in recent conversations Stu Lang was talking about establishing the Lang Debates, similar to the Munk Debates, which would focus on business as a force for good. Such ideas, Moreton adds, dovetail with the work and outlook of Armstrong and Lucky Iron Fish.

Moreton offers up one last example to reinforce the reputation of Guelph as a caring school. He points to current university president Charlotte Yates, who is committed to community diversity and student support.

"I was sitting with her, and I asked, what would the news release at the end of your presidency say, what would you want it to read?" Moreton says. "And right away she said she wanted it to be about student mental health and wellness. She wants to be known in terms of bringing in a lot more support and being a leader in that area. Other university presidents might be more interested in having brought in a new engineering building or stadium. It was pretty telling that she came up with that right away."

Against that cultural backdrop at the University of Guelph, more life-changing moments followed for Armstrong. In 2011, he went to Dadaab in Kenya, the world's largest refugee camp. This was during his first year as a master's student working on international development, which included taking on a fundraising initiative as a volunteer for the Shine the Light Campaign and the World University Service of Canada. Security concerns were part of the equation at

Dadaab. Aid workers were often kidnapped. Armstrong had already arrived in Kenya when famine was officially declared in the Horn of Africa. The Canadian government had sent a delegation to help. "One of the memories that stayed with me was being in this long queue to get in because of the various admission processes," Armstrong recalls. "They have to test to see if you have health and identification documents. Identify profiles. They are screening on the ground for refugees to be admitted. A mother was holding a child who had died, and they tried to indicate there was nothing they could do to help. It was quite difficult. Another woman was trying to get in and her face was covered, I assume for religious reasons. They were trying to get a photograph and she was refusing. They ripped it off. She was trapped. She gave up everything, including her religious beliefs, just to have access."

After entering the camp, they were then shown a burial site on the outskirts of Dadaab, where refugees carried their dead to be put to rest. It was heart-wrenching.

Armstrong returned to Canada knowing that he wanted to do more fundraising to address these international issues. One of his initiatives was founding the Guelph chapter of Universities Fighting World Hunger. The group was a network of university chapters that originated out of Auburn University in Alabama. Through it, Armstrong met Dr. June Henton, a professor and dean of Auburn's College of Human Sciences since 1985. Now retired, Henton became one of Armstrong's most influential mentors, and he maintains a special relationship with her.

Armstrong had other work to do. In 2011, he organized a summit on Guelph's campus. Students from all over North America came to educate themselves on hunger issues and how they could be solved. At the end of the event, everyone participating had to make a commitment about what they would be doing to address the issues one year later.

"Mine was to provide more resources for people suffering from hunger," says Armstrong.

He acted. Armstrong organized a world-record meal-packing event on the U of G campus during Orientation Week, which was part of the university's BetterPlanet Project. Approximately two thousand members of the university and surrounding community gathered to pack over 315,000 emergency relief meals in one hour. It was 115,000 more than the goal. The volunteers met in the university's field house and created an assembly line to measure and pack the meals, which contained rice, soy, vegetables, beans, and a vitamin packet sealed in plastic bags with the BetterPlanet Project logo emblazoned on them.

The aforementioned Whitfield pointed to Armstrong's loyalty as a defining characteristic, in both his professional and personal lives. She was privy to this passion when they attended the University of Guelph together. Whitfield recalls the commitment he had after returning from the refugee camp.

"Gavin takes that passion and moves it into action," she says, citing the meal-packing event as an example. "He has no fear of dreaming big, which I think is commendable. He doesn't waste a moment."

A partnership was formed with American non-governmental organizations: Outreach and ONExONE, which helped distribute the meals to Mauritania, one of Africa's poorest countries, which had been devastated by drought. In the wake of this activity, Armstrong became the first Canadian to receive the President William Jefferson Clinton Hunger Leadership Award.

"We had people from across campus and in the community," he says of the meal-packing activity. "It was important to have that interaction. It was the first-year students' introduction to Guelph, and it was a really cool way to show how engaged the city was and how tight-knit the community was.

"We were put into the Guinness World Records according to the volume we produced over sixty minutes." His group organized two more such events, and over the three years combined the community packaged more than one million emergency relief meals. The meal-packing effort included fundraising that brought in about $250,000 over the three years.

The long list of work and achievements throughout his university career wasn't what Armstrong had in mind when he came to Guelph. The plan to be a wealthy banker had completely shifted. Experiential learning sent him on a different path and opened doors. Armstrong was defining himself in the process.

"His journey as a student shows growth and evolution," notes Lang. "You're developing your personal brand, and this is one of the things I remember talking about quite a bit with students in class. We talk about products and services, but we are walking billboards. We are our own brand, essentially comprised of our integrity, our character, and our values, not just the clothes we wear.

"When we describe who Gavin is, the brand he has become, and what he is known for, that growth happens with every student at any university. At some point, you come into your own and recognize that you can diversify your interests."

"Gavin was a student who was really charting his own path," adds Dr. Julia Christensen Hughes, the president of Yorkville University in Toronto and former dean of the Lang School of Business and Economics at the University of Guelph. "He was looking to take advantage of innovative learning opportunities."

Christensen Hughes points out that Armstrong's first-year seminar course with Summerlee really emboldened those students and exposed them to what learning looks like at its best. They were in small groups, using problem-based learning with the freedom to ask questions and explore.

"As a business student, Gavin brought that learning to his courses, while seeking alternatives to a traditional path," she recalls. "I was very supportive of that. I love the concept of encouraging students to explore innovative electives and different kinds of learning opportunities. He really embraced that.

"He told the story, and I love it, that he was coming to study business to be an investment banker so he could make a lot of money. He was coming to study business to put himself on that life path. But along the way, he really came to understand the power of education. Gavin equipped himself to help change the world for the better, and from a business point of view, to embrace this notion of business as a force of good."

In a way, Armstrong influenced Christensen Hughes. When she was being considered for the role of dean, that idea of businesses doing good was a core belief she held. The Lang School of Business and Economics embraced the idea of developing leaders for a sustainable world. Students like Armstrong.

In 2012, he dropped his master's quest to take on a new and unconventional challenge, with the switch directly to a Ph.D. in biomedical science. He knew he needed to expand the scope of his education. The change to the Ph.D. was to facilitate taking over the research of Charles, as outlined earlier. Charles was moving on to medical school and handed off his work on the Happy Fish to Armstrong, after which it evolved to Lucky Iron Fish. The move brought on a steep learning curve for someone who had not done much on the science front in some time. Armstrong read voraciously and used tutors to help get through the work.

It was while doing his research that Armstrong began to determine that there could be a commercial opportunity and he actually launched Lucky Iron Fish while still working on his Ph.D.

Working toward his doctorate required delivering a presentation and an oral examination that focused on iron deficiency and the biomedical science related to it. He then conducted research and completed his thesis: "Commercializing the Lucky Iron Fish™ Using Social Enterprise: A Novel Health Innovation for Iron Deficiency and Anemia in Cambodia and Beyond."

With Lucky Iron Fish in position to combat the alarming rate of iron deficiency in Cambodians, Armstrong's approach was rare. In most cases, thesis research is completed first and commercialization follows. Armstrong, in his maverick way, wanted to consider the commercialization component of his social business as it happened, as his thesis evolved.

He travelled to Phnom Penh.

"I wanted there to be a positive social impact embedded in every aspect of this business," Armstrong explains. "It wasn't just the fish helping people but also how we got the fish out to the people. That included employment, environmental footprint, our commitment to social causes and equality, and supporting local organizations.

"The [second] packaging for the units was recycled palm leaves done by Cambodian women. They had had a challenging history and we felt compelled to do as much as we could to help them."

Auburn's Henton was initially doubtful of Armstrong's decision to enter a Ph.D. program, given his academic background.

"I wondered how he could take that on," Henton says. "But he proved all of us wrong and came through with flying colours, not only finishing his Ph.D. but also marketing Lucky Iron Fish at the same time. It was truly an amazing success story."

When he began the transformation from craving riches to helping others in need, various observers point out, the true Gavin Armstrong came out, the one with compassion, empathy, and the ability to love. Others have noticed.

"Gavin's personal development over the years has been amazing," says Lloyd Longfield, the Liberal Member of Parliament for Guelph and formerly head of the local Chamber of Commerce.

"There's confidence, he's smiling. He has transformed from a shy person who had been bullied, with no confidence. He has done good in the world and his business has been good for him. That's the success of his story, what his business has done for his personal development so that he can now go out and support other people."

Longfield references a book where the author argues, "When you're looking out for other people, you have a purpose for living. The reason is something beyond you."

"I would say that Gavin has found real meaning in that way," Longfield concludes.

The Lucky Iron Fish, branded with a Canadian maple leaf, along with its protection oil. This is the bundle that is available for sale online.

This cool glass of sangria reflects the wide variety of ways a Lucky Iron Fish can be put to use.

Christopher Charles conducting research in Cambodia.

Christopher Charles in rural Cambodia, where he lived for a short period of time.

Young Cambodian girls holding the Lucky Iron Fish.

Early packaging for the Lucky Iron Fish along with its original logo.

Gavin Armstrong being recognized by Chelsea Clinton at the Clinton Global Initiative University.

Gavin Armstrong receiving the University of Guelph Alumni Medal of Achievement. Several years earlier he'd thought he would never be able to graduate. From left to right: Armstrong; Karen Kuwahara, honoured for volunteerism; university president Franco Vaccarino; and Dr. Harry Brightwell, University of Guelph Alumni of Honour Award winner.

A bike carrying fruit in rural Cambodia, a common sight.

The original production method for the fish in Kandal Province, Cambodia. This family produced the original units.

The Lucky Iron Leaf, or Lucky Shakti Leaf, was developed for vegetarian communities.

Gavin Armstrong celebrating the partnership agreement with Industrial Metal Powders (IMP) in Pune, India. The company now produces the Lucky Iron Fish for LIFe's global sales.

The Lucky Iron Fish team in 2019, from left to right: Linda Armstrong, Yogendra Kalavalapalli, Shraddha Sekhon, Angela McMonagle, Gavin Armstrong, Anne Pringle, Stephanie Bergeron, Melissa Saunders, and Jamie Lee.

Gavin Armstrong presenting his commitment to action at the Clinton Global Initiative University (CGIU) along with fellow student leaders and President Clinton in 2015. In 2011, Armstrong was the First Canadian to receive the President William Jefferson Clinton Hunger Leadership Award. Photo courtesy of Clinton Global Initiative University (CGIU).

Schoolchildren holding the Lucky Iron Fish in Cambodia. This school was a recipient of donated units.

The Lucky Iron Fish displayed against the background of a typical village in rural Cambodia.

A schoolchild holding the Lucky Iron Fish in Cambodia.

Gavin Armstrong speaking about entrepreneurship at a session in Guelph.

Community recipients in Tanzania displaying the Lucky Iron Fish.

Kids with the Lucky Iron Fish in Cambodia.

Lucky Iron Fish units being distributed with partner CARE Benin/Togo in Benin. The program was run in partnership with CARE International and funded by the Canadian Fund for Innovation and Transformation (FIT).

A woman participating in a Lucky Iron Fish pilot program in Tanzania.

A mother with a child displays the Lucky Iron Fish in Tanzania.

Soup being prepared with a Lucky Iron Fish.

Gavin Armstrong (centre) along with team members Tania Framst (left) and Anne Pringle (right) in Tanzania.

The Lucky Iron Fish being distributed to a community in Benin.

On Parliament Hill in Ottawa, GlobalMedic and volunteers pack Lucky Iron Fish into family emergency kits destined for Somalia.

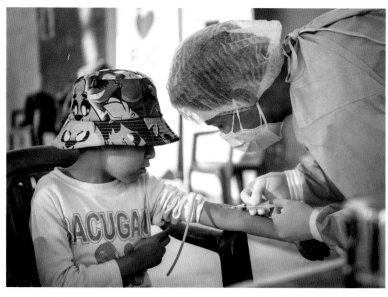

Blood sample being taken by NGO partner EUG Arequipa in Peru in 2022.

Team member Anne Pringle in Hong Kong at a Leaders to Leaders Summit in 2018.

Gavin Armstrong prior to filming his appearance on *Dragons' Den*.

A woman cooking with a fish in Benin in 2022. Photo courtesy of CARE Benin.

The Lucky Iron Fish team had to adjust to a hybrid working model due to the Covid-19 pandemic. Here, in 2023, clockwise from left, are Tegan Mosugu (on screen), Shraddha Sekhon (on screen), and from left to right Anne Pringle, Linda Armstrong, Melissa Saunders, Stephanie Bergeron, and Gavin Armstrong.

# Chapter 5

# Early Life of LIFe

WHILE ARMSTRONG'S PERSONAL growth blossomed during his time at the University of Guelph, his research and related work at the institution also were fundamental to the development and early years of Lucky Iron Fish.

One of the helpful factors in the development of this social enterprise was a fortuitous connection to Auburn University in Alabama. It was back in 2006–7, says Harriet Giles, at the time director of external relations at the school. She says the dean of her college (the College of Human Sciences), the aforementioned June Henton, received a call from the dean of veterinary medicine at Auburn, who was hosting Guelph president Summerlee and suggested she and Giles come over to meet him because he was very interested in global challenges.

"And then when we heard that Guelph had been given the title of the most caring university in the world, we obviously could see why, just in talking to him and his passion for changing the world," Giles recalls, noting that Auburn had been at the core of Universities Fighting World Hunger. "He said right on the spot, when we told him about the hunger efforts, he said he would like to work with us and hoped to become the Canadian arm."

Summerlee was invited to attend a subsequent Universities Fighting World Hunger conference, and he had Armstrong tag along with him.

"And that's how we met Gavin and immediately we clicked with him," Giles says. "Gavin just embraced the university's world hunger movement, and he went back to Guelph and got a group going there to support us and become involved. Then the University of Guelph hosted a Universities Fighting World Hunger conference, and Gavin organized it. Nobody's ever raised something like the $140,000 he raised for that conference."

Because the conference was in February, Giles said it was a "lovely, lovely, lovely Canadian winter for me, it was one of the coldest winters for Canada. Can you imagine people from Alabama with our thin wool coats coming up there then? But it was so much fun." And the ties with Armstrong were strengthened.

Auburn's Hunger Solutions Institute (HSI) named four HSI fellows, and Armstrong was one of them.

"He stayed at Auburn a good bit of the time and worked on Lucky Iron Fish during that time," Giles continues. "So we obviously proudly claimed Gavin as one of ours in that Lucky Iron Fish had a strong association with Universities Fighting World Hunger. He did represent Guelph, but he was also a Fulbright fellow, and he took his Fulbright and came to Auburn. And so we very proudly say that we have an association with Lucky Iron Fish through Gavin and his affiliation, spending part of his Fulbright year at Auburn and also being one of our HSI fellows."

Armstrong explains he applied for the Fulbright because it is a prestigious honour and would allow him to conduct research in an international network.

Both Giles and Henton were invited by Armstrong to be on the Lucky Iron Fish advisory board.

"Gavin's a treasured friend and certainly a valued colleague in all that we've done, and I just couldn't be happier for him to see him succeed," Giles concludes.

There are substantial local plaudits as well.

Guelph MP Longfield first connected with Armstrong when the former was interested in innovation. As head of the Guelph Chamber of Commerce at the time, he oversaw the move of the office to a building overseen by Innovation Guelph. Startups would work there to develop their pitches, and among the startups was Armstrong's.

"He wanted to try to develop this solution for developing countries," Longfield recalls. "Social innovation was something we were very interested in, along with the fact it was coming out of the University of Guelph and commercialization. We were providing some mentorship for the business planning, marketing, and execution. And we were helping make some connections for Gavin that would help him launch the product. We had a few trade shows and tech showcases at Innovation Guelph where he was able to have a trade booth set up."

Longfield now has a vantage point on the enterprise as a federal Member of Parliament, and he notes that Lucky Iron Fish aligns well with the government's goals for Africa and all developing countries.

Building on the evolutionary research undertaken by Charles, Armstrong was immersed in his education while envisioning and planning commercial possibilities; eventually it would all come together.

"While also advancing the science, he was committed to doing a graduate degree, and this is another thing that is brilliant about Gavin in both his undergraduate and graduate degree," notes Christensen Hughes, who was dean of business at Guelph when Armstrong was there. "He actually embraced a model that I think is the future of education, but he invented it for himself. And he ran into a lot of institutional hurdles. I mean, universities are not the most elastic when it comes to their rules, but he found this incredible way to earn academic credit.

"And he still managed to pursue his Ph.D. And with Alastair [Summerlee] on his committee, Gavin was doing pretty rigorous and intense scientific analysis. They wanted to take the proof to the next level, working with folks at other universities and NGOs. But his was a very unique Ph.D., where not only was he moving forward the scientific evidence of the efficacy, but he was also creating a new business model of social enterprise.

"When I talk about this stuff, some people I think get the impression that I'm a business school dean who doesn't understand the necessity of profits, but profit is not a dirty word. Profits are core to the concept of a sustainable business model. But the idea is that the three Ps that we're caring about are people, caring about the planet, and caring about profit. So it's about holding those concepts in balance, so that business as a force for good can continue."

Christensen Hughes has provided support in other ways for Armstrong and Lucky Iron Fish. For example, a couple of years ago, when the business's board was wrestling over different strategic directions, she was invited to lead a process for the board to work through the challenges. In light of the overall development, she describes herself as a cheerleader and fan.

In those early days, Armstrong was interested in the work Charles was doing and helped in the production of a video for a grant application.

"Chris was the one who originated the concept of the iron disk that was shaped like a fish, and he had called it Happy Fish, which was the name of his thesis," Armstrong recalls. "He was looking to graduate, and he wanted to go to medical school and not continue the work but he wanted the research to still go on. I had applied to the university to further the work, do clinical trials on it, and then eventually commercialize it. Chris wanted to go to med school, but he knew that there was something important in the concept, it just needed to be continued."

Friction can be common when the mentor of a product hands it off to others for commercialization. Charles and Armstrong worked to address this, and Charles has sat on the board for numerous terms and given input into the growth, strategy, and evolution of Lucky Iron Fish. He also has founding equity in the company.

"I actually went to Cambodia in late 2011 to visit and hear more about the work he was doing. It was my first time going to Cambodia," Armstrong recalls.

The position that Armstrong pursued was promoted through Charles and Summerlee, and only a few people applied. In his undergrad, Armstrong's focus had been on social business or corporate social responsibility, which gave him the perspective to see a possible commercial opportunity for the fish. At the time, it seemed to make sense for Cambodia, with the possibility that the business could eventually be expanded geographically. Ultimately, Armstrong created the business based in Canada, largely because doing so in Cambodia would have been a challenge.

Armstrong had to establish a research design that would continue to validate the efficacy of the product and that met the standards for a Ph.D. program. For initial financing he applied for money from the University of Guelph, which had commercialization grants. That was adequate for getting the ball rolling, then Armstrong applied for Grand Challenges Canada funding for the research itself, and he received five hundred thousand dollars.

"The first thing we had to do was design and conduct a clinical trial to address feedback from other clinical trials," Armstrong explains. "It was all very promising but there were limitations, and the international nutrition community wanted to see further evidence, so designing and conducting trials was important. So that was step one.

"There were some Lucky Iron Fish in existence, but they were flawed. They were made from various sources of iron, so the quality was inconsistent. They were very prone to rust, and they broke easily, and at the end of the day you couldn't produce a quantity that would be needed to grow a program. So we had to identify and create a reliable product. And ultimately it ended up being successful.

"In terms of producing the units, it took me a very long time to source iron that was contaminant-free, and I had to establish a memorandum of understanding with the Royal University of Phnom Penh to test every batch to make sure they were safe.

"I applied to do the Ph.D. and started in September, but then I started outlining what my thesis was going to look like. I wanted half of the thesis to be on the science of the fish. So it would be about the efficacy, the safety, and that this was a viable solution," Armstrong says. "But then I wanted half of it to be on creating a social business."

One of the challenges at the beginning was that he sought to commercialize the Lucky Iron Fish right away, which led to immediate challenges on the credibility of the product — critics suggested there was a built-in bias because the business would make money on the product.

"The normal trajectory is you do the research, you publish it, and then you commercialize it. But you can't tell me anyone who's doing research isn't planning on commercializing it and therefore making money on it. It was the case that we made our intentions clear from the beginning, whereas other people would have just waited until it was done. It felt a little bit unfair in that way."

To expedite product development and business growth, Armstrong moved to Cambodia in late 2012.

"When I was first there, before we could do any clinical trials or any work, we had to actually make a product," Armstrong continues. "Chris had sourced some iron, and it was easy to make thirty or fifty of them. But the costs weren't really efficient."

With that challenge, Armstrong started hunting for another source of iron. However, language limitations and inadequate technology made the task difficult. Trying to have fruitful discussions with locals about metallurgy was never easy, and Google Maps wasn't effective, so Armstrong was regularly lost.

"One weekend I went on a guided bike tour, and our guide, Davuth, was really nice. He spoke English really well," Armstrong recalls. "He had done his master's in social work in Hawaii, and he said he was looking at leaving his job. So I just said, 'Do you want to work for me? I need some help.' And so he did. He helped find sources of iron and acted as a translator, and he had a connection with the Royal University of Phnom Penh."

Armstrong was able to work with the university's lab to do the quality analysis of the iron. He and his new team member would find sources of iron and bring them to the lab, and if the samples had any contaminants in them, such as arsenic, mercury, or lead, they were not usable. Ultimately, they found iron that was suitable — interestingly enough, it was sourced from automotive brake pads. This worked because unlike much of the iron in Cambodia, which has high arsenic content, the brake pads were made in South Korea and were contaminant-free.

The next step was to find a processing company, and eventually they made contact with a family firm that made metal products such as tools and manhole covers.

The company was located out in a rural province, so they took the eighty-minute drive in a tuk-tuk (a motorized, three-wheeled taxi) and met with them. The processors came up with different shapes and iterations of the product, and after some trial and error the team was able to determine how much iron was being leached into the water. With that information in hand, they needed to settle on a size for the product.

"A convex shape helps the iron fish roll in the pot, so it had to have this certain convexness to it," Armstrong explains. "And so the company started making the fish for us in the ground. They made these moulds and they put them in the dirt and then they melted the iron in this big pot using fire."

Between 2012 and 2014, they built up a large inventory of the fish using this process. Since at the time Armstrong felt the business was going to be based only in Cambodia, he kept production and packaging there, and he put a sales team and a marketing strategy in place.

"But no one was buying the product, because we weren't really trusted. The concept was too foreign, and the fish weren't selling," Armstrong recalls. "But at the same time, I was speaking about what we were doing internationally at conferences. I was travelling and speaking about it and people would come up to me and say, 'I love this, can I buy one because I have iron deficiency?'"

Those instances prodded a change in thinking that recognized there was an international market for the product, so the company started selling the units online out of Canada and they identified a production foundry in Ontario to make the units that could be sold globally.

"It wasn't just mistrust in Cambodia," Armstrong points out. "It was such an unusual concept, so it took more than one house call to make a sale. You really had to establish yourself, you had to get buy-in from village elders, community leaders, and that took time. The investment you had to make just to make a sale was expensive. What we ended up doing was shift our business model. We partnered with aid organizations that were already established on the ground, so they already had trust within the community, village leaders knew why they were there, and that's when uptake really took off."

The team needed to understand the acceptability of the original fish, so they used it in focus group testing, during which Armstrong kept hearing the same phrase over and over. Davuth explained that the participants were not calling the product the "lucky" iron fish, but instead something like the heavy black fish.

"And why would they call it lucky?" Armstrong says. "It looks like a heavy black fish." In the locals' language, *lucky* is a very complicated word, "so we put the symbol for *good* on the fish, and they called it the 'good fish.' I was okay with that. The new batch of the fish had the word *good* on them. And that's the batch that we used for the clinical trial."

The trials themselves lasted a year, and then it took six to eight months to do the analysis after the fact.

Steps such as sourcing iron, designing, and testing were challenges in their own right, and as the process moved forward more difficulties arose. Since Armstrong was commercializing the product, the criticisms of bias were ever-present, which emphasized the need for continued clinical trials and required partnering with researchers from other universities.

While the trials were going on, Armstrong was working at creating awareness for the project and developing a business plan for Cambodia, noting that there was sufficient confidence in the original research. That effort included presenting at various academic conferences, as was stipulated as a requirement for his Ph.D. That effort took him to nutrition conferences around the world.

For the new trial itself, he and his team chose a different province in Cambodia. This province was located in a different region of the country from where the previous work was conducted, and it had reported higher rates of iron deficiency.

"We wanted to show some diversity in diet and location," Armstrong explains. "One of the challenges in Chris's trial was during the rainy season; the product worked, but it stopped working or worked to a lesser rate in the dry season. That's because people were using well water in the dry season, and there's arsenic in the ground and arsenic binds iron.

"When we got the results from the new trial, we saw that the fish didn't really have an impact on the users' iron status, but neither did supplements. When we collected our midline data, we also did genetic testing to look for any genetic abnormalities, and we found that the majority of the population did have iron deficiency anemia, but they also had thalassemia."

While they were initially shocked by the results, identifying the thalassemia issue made sense. Thalassemia is a blood disorder where the body doesn't produce enough hemoglobin, which is an important part of red blood cells. Iron supplements and iron fortification don't solve thalassemia.

"So you wouldn't expect the fish to work, and it didn't," says Armstrong. "But the positive outcome from that study is that it also didn't cause any toxicity in the population. So we learned that the fish is only effective at treating iron deficiency and iron deficiency anemia, but not other forms of anemia such as thalassemia.

"I have learned a lot about running clinical trials and the need for diverse data. As of 2023 there were over twenty clinical trials or research projects conducted around the world that demonstrate the efficacy of the fish. We always partner with independent institutions to run the work to help eliminate any perception of bias.

"But the challenge is that some researchers said this [finding related to thalassemia] proves the fish doesn't work at all, and that that means the other studies didn't work," he explains. "I continued to do more research, and I got funding and was getting research institutions on board. That's when we began testing in other countries to positive effect.

"There are some skeptics who believe that our product doesn't work, and they'll blog about it, write to the media, and write to companies who partner with us, and say, 'You know, I did a study with them that proves it doesn't work.' And we've noted numerous times that we've done fifteen other studies that prove that it does."

Armstrong continued in Cambodia until 2014, trying to establish the business, confident there was plenty of data that demonstrated the product worked, and he acknowledges some of his confidence was misplaced. He had begun fully engaging with the international nutrition community and ultimately agreed that stronger data was needed.

"We met with NGOs who work in areas such as food security and health care, and they all said that there's not enough [supporting] data," Armstrong says. "And then I tried to [go back to selling] the product door to door and people said, 'I don't know why I would buy this. I get iron supplements for free from the government and who are you?' So we only sold a handful of fish. It didn't really work."

Then in 2014 he spoke at a conference in the U.S. After the talk a throng of people approached him to try to buy the fish because they had iron deficiency. The experience was an eye-opener for Armstrong, because he had convinced himself that no one in North America would use the product. He had seen it only as having South Asian application, perhaps adding Thailand and Malaysia after Cambodia. That's when the idea of selling online started to gain momentum, so the team built a website and they began selling globally in 2015. Still, they knew they faced an important hurdle in that they had to make sure they had all approvals in place and were following government regulations.

"We actually started selling pins. If you bought a pin for yourself online, we would buy a fish for a family in Cambodia," he says. "That's how we were trying to grow the Cambodian business. People bought them. It was simply a pin that looked like the fish — I still always wear them when I'm speaking. And it was all out of my basement."

With approval eventually secured to sell in Canada, Armstrong started hauling the fish back to Canada in suitcases, which he admits was not a very efficient way to transport the product. "I broke a lot of suitcases." This iteration of the fish also incorporated its first packaging, which was made by an NGO in Cambodia from recycled newspaper.

"One time our translator looked really uncomfortable," Armstrong recalls. The translator was looking at the wrapper on one of the fish. "I asked what was wrong. And he said, 'This is about a murder, a newspaper story about a brutal murder or a car accident or something.' I couldn't read the paper. If people could understand Khmer, you would understand what the article was saying. So then we moved to have the packaging made from recycled palm leaf, so it was biodegradable. And it was produced by a co-operative that hired Cambodians living with disabilities. A lot of the women who worked there were landmine victims. So we produced these cool boxes."

Armstrong takes pride in the social and environmental aspects of the business, this packaging stage being a prime example.

At some point, a BBC stringer in Cambodia had latched on to the story of the iron fish and iron deficiency. They had even interviewed Armstrong, and then ran a story about it in May 2017.

"It was a long weekend, so I was sleeping in. I woke up to some missed calls. And our inbox was flooded, and they were all sales," Armstrong recalls. "At first I thought we had been hacked! We did not have enough product. We were able to get some fish mailed to us, and we were working in a little office in Guelph, Ontario, doing the packaging ourselves and mailing them out. That's when we realized that the production capacity wasn't really adequate.

"But I was thrilled. I mean, I love the BBC," Armstrong says. "I didn't know the story would have this impact. We sold out." Global demand for the product continued to grow.

"Whenever I spoke, either during the question-and-answer or after the presentation, I would have a lineup of people come up to me and say, 'I have iron deficiency. This is amazing. Can I buy one?

Where can I get one?'" Armstrong says. "I'd have to say, 'Oh, I don't have any.' I realized that if people wanted this in London or New York or wherever I was speaking, maybe there was a global demand for this. That's when we went to selling the Lucky Iron Fish globally.

"So I went back to Cambodia to try to perfect the supply chain. It was really challenging to figure everything out. You couldn't run an e-commerce business from Cambodia, at least at that time, and everything became kind of a bit of a headache." Armstrong wanted to continue to have the packaging done in Cambodia, because he welcomed the social aspect of the co-operative they were working with. However, the organization was unable to produce at the volume required. They tried another organization, one that used recycled cardboard and vegetable ink, but they still could not get the quality they wanted for the packaging, so they found a Canadian firm in Bowmanville to produce the fish and packaging, and assembly was done in Guelph.

"We had the boxes printed, and then to assemble them we used a charity in Guelph that hired people with learning disabilities and who perhaps had difficulty finding work," Armstrong says. "They made furniture and did construction and woodworking and things like that. So we actually hired this organization to do the kitting. Again, we wanted to have a social impact, where if we were having to spend money, we were going to spend it on a nice organization."

That lasted for a period but unfortunately the organization doing the kitting was heavily reliant on grants, and when their funding was lost, they went out of business. In fact, one of the goals of a trip Armstrong made to India in 2020 was to try to identify an organization there to do the packaging, since the manufacturing had been moved to India in 2018. However, in a terrible twist of fate, Covid-19 shutdowns began during the trip, and he ended up having to cancel a number of meetings — so the packaging is still done in Canada.

While Armstrong was doing his Fulbright scholarship at Auburn, he had the idea to turn the smile on the fish into an indicator for how long the fish lasts. He worked with an engineer to determine the required depth of the smile so that it would fade away after five years of regular use, indicating to users it was time to get a new fish.

In shifting the manufacturing of the fish to a company in India in 2018, much trial and error was still required. Initially the fish were really sharp, and the ones being distributed were rusting. The producers responded by coating the units in oil, but they arrived in a grotesque state requiring extensive cleaning. Eventually the manufacturer steamed the fish after they made them to prevent rust.

Against the backdrop of startup obstacles, it would be wrong to assume that being a gay entrepreneur would not come with its own challenges. Armstrong says the odds were stacked against him.

"Seven out of ten startups fail in the first three years," he says. "Then you add being from an underrepresented group, there's the added level of discrimination that you can face. I have experienced that. At the beginning, I hid it. It felt like going back into the closet. I was just very aware of how I was talking, what I was wearing, how I was doing my hair, my mannerisms. So much energy was going into how I was portraying myself, I wasn't actually focused on the objective, which was raising money.

"Conversations in front of investors are when you're the most vulnerable, because you're seeking money to support your business, and it's their money. As an entrepreneur, I'm the boss, so I'm okay with how my employees, stakeholders, production team, or the media see me. But investors hold a lot of control. So that's why I am very cautious of how I present myself. And I found that it was actually making me a little depressed, because it did feel like I was going back in the closet."

He is reminded of the discrimination he experienced. In one case an individual was looking to invest, and the meetings had gone well. Then they wrote to say they had gone through Armstrong's social media and discovered posts that didn't align with their values.

"Examples were posts of me on a beach, and I was in a Speedo or small bathing suit versus surf trunks," he related. "That's like a dog whistle for homophobic people."

It was around this time that Armstrong came across the Canadian Gay and Lesbian Chamber of Commerce (CGLCC). He found it refreshing to discover an organization made up of gay entrepreneurs. Armstrong joined formally in 2020.

"For somebody so young, he has a great story to share already," notes Darrell Schuurman, co-founder and chief executive officer of the CGLCC, which today is called Canada's 2SLGBTQI+ Chamber of Commerce. The organization was formed in 2003, when the Canadian founders had been working closely with colleagues in the U.S. who had started a similar chamber the year before, triggering plans to start a national body in Canada.

"My sense is that he probably struggled a little bit with being gay, and he had problems or struggles growing up, so I think for him, seeing this business organization with its purpose to support people like him, who are also passionate about entrepreneurship, that are passionate about business, was positive," Schuurman says. "I think it opened his eyes a little bit and exposed him to a different community than he was used to."

The chamber offers a variety of support for entrepreneurs like Armstrong, from advisory help to general support.

"I think at the core, it's about helping to connect," Schuurman explains. "But I think it hopefully hits a range of advantages and helps to create those connections with other LGBTQ businesses, with corporate partners, and with government agencies."

Schuurman first connected with Armstrong at an Ernst & Young Entrepreneur of the Year awards gala in 2017.

"He was the recipient of, I think it was, social entrepreneur of the year," Schuurman notes. "He was on stage in front of maybe three thousand people, and he outwardly thanked his partner. And because he thanked his same-sex partner on stage, you know he's somebody that identifies as being gay. He was a business owner, entrepreneur, successful, and was clearly very passionate about what he was doing. It was at that moment that I thought, 'I've got to have a conversation with him.'"

Schuurman shares two observations.

"First you have somebody who's relatively young going out and building a successful business. I always found that really fascinating. And then, just Lucky Iron Fish alone, the story is, what you can say? It's just such a great and moving story. It's hard not to become passionate about this, and for me, it's about creating change and saving lives. Clearly, Lucky Iron Fish and Gavin are having a huge impact on the world."

One of the key people at Lucky Iron Fish is Anne Pringle, who joined in 2018 after running her own business. In fact, it was because of that business that she connected with Armstrong, when they both went through a business incubator together. With a partner, Pringle had started a sustainable, ethical clothing business, but closed it in 2014.

"In my role with Lucky Iron Fish I was very excited, because part of it is impact measurement, and that's something I'm really passionate about," she says. "Pretty much my entire career has been with social enterprise and social impact, so it's very exciting to be in this role. Part of what I do is help distribute the impact fund, which started as a buy one, give one program but evolved right into a new fund where we put a portion of money from each sale into a fund. It involves working with partners, in Canada and around the world, to distribute fish and resources, and then also working on a larger scale with NGOs to purchase directly from us, and then we co-create programming that makes sense for the community where we're working."

Pringle notes that Lucky Iron Fish is a small part of the global health sector but adds that food inequality and its impact know no boundaries.

"We see it even here in Canada," she says. "We work with food banks and local organizations, under the understanding that Toronto is the child poverty capital of Canada — there are so many houses that are food insecure in our cities. In our roles we see it around the world, and we're just really getting to understand more and more about our food systems and inequalities. I think one of the things that is helpful is the number of really incredible people that we've met and organizations here in Canada or around the world that are doing really fantastic work within their communities. And it's been very interesting, I think, from conferences, for example, to see that there's this global recognition that it's moving forward. Communities know the best solution within their community."

Lucky Iron Fish works with organizations that help people with iron deficiency as well as a whole host of other issues that they may experience, too. Pringle points to an organization based in India that started in the 1970s. It has worked with HIV-positive individuals dealing with substance abuse and other health challenges.

"First, they were working with men, but then they realized they need to also work with women," she adds. "And they've evolved this into a really incredible organization that works within the community. They have a local care home, and they also have an ambulance of sorts that goes out into the community and delivers health care. But it expands beyond that, because we've worked with a number of women who have become widowed because their partner has died due to complications around HIV or TB. Many of these women have had to turn to sex work, and many have faced sexual assault on multiple occasions.

"And they're also iron deficient and facing other forms of nutrient deficiencies, and they're raising children. So, this organization does this really phenomenal, holistic approach to the work that they do. I've gotten to know the executive director quite well through some of our work and she's one of the most inspiring people I've ever met in my life. They take an approach where most of the people who now work there were first clients of the work that they did, so they understand so intimately the problems that the community is facing, and they approach them without judgment, there's no stigma. I find it incredibly inspiring and rewarding, but it is also emotionally heavy, meeting women and hearing their stories."

A vegetarian through a large portion of her life, Pringle acknowledges she has struggled with iron deficiency and says that she understands the symptoms at a high level. It's through Lucky Iron Fish that she truly grasps how complicated the deficiency really is, and how far-reaching it is around the world.

"It really hits home when we start saying how beneficial it also is for children and cognitive development," she continues. "That's a thread throughout every place we work, whether it's Canada, or Tanzania, or India, or Guatemala, it's that people are so committed to helping their children. A lot of what we get is anecdotal feedback — 'I can see my child's energy improved,' or 'They're doing better in school.' And that's always really lovely to hear. So the long-term goal is we want to see iron deficiency reduced around the world. We want to see, as a result of that, symptoms decreasing, from headaches and nausea to fainting, while also improving cognitive development."

In some of the Lucky Iron Fish work in East and West Africa, they conduct a train-the-trainer program, working directly with community health care workers, perhaps the staff at an NGO, or some ministry of health officials. This program trains people about Lucky Iron Fish and how to implement best practices for delivering a program in a community. In some cases they go into a community with health care workers who do the training, and Lucky Iron Fish representatives can provide feedback.

Pringle points out that during the peak of the Covid-19 pandemic, much of their work had to be done remotely, which was a challenge because being in person always makes it easier to train people and develop a close bond with the organizations you're working with. Optimistically, however, she sees a better understanding evolving of how effectively connecting digitally can deliver benefits.

"Maybe our work won't involve as much travelling around the world anymore, because we'll develop really strong mechanisms to communicate virtually," she speculates. "And I think that can move us toward greater sustainability, with less flying overall."

As Covid-19 was gaining a foothold globally, Pringle was in Peru. Then she was back in Canada for two days before heading out on that fateful trip to India with Gavin, during which Covid-19 shutdowns began in earnest and many of their plans had to be cancelled. Lucky Iron Fish had identified India as one of two countries, along with Peru, where it might significantly scale up its work. Iron deficiency is a large problem in both countries, and each one had instituted programs to address anemia, including large-scale programs working with children and women of reproductive age. Many people were using iron pills, but there were also a lot of other interventions, such as micronutrient powders, syrups, or iron salts.

"We thought these countries, based on the research we had done, made a lot of sense as places for us to scale up," Pringle says. "In Peru, we were able to host two events. It was great; the Canadian embassy was really supportive. We brought together NGOs, corporations, social enterprises, all working in iron deficiency in some capacity, and we presented our research. Peru was a great kickoff point to get in front of so many organizations.

"But both India and Peru were hard hit by Covid-19, and in places where iron deficiency was already a problem, iron-rich foods can be more expensive, meats can be more expensive. So we know there will be long-term impacts of this. We're looking at how we partner right now and work with organizations so we can move into how we can work with organizations within the endemic stage of Covid-19 when the timing is right."

As the global battle against Covid-19 became sustained over time, steps were put in place to maintain the viability of the business (discussed in more detail in Chapter 7). The Toronto-based sales team operates essentially via e-commerce, either through the Lucky Iron Fish website or Amazon.

Armstrong explains that the business moved to remote as a result of Covid-19. Lucky Iron Fish shut its physical office down in 2020 in one of the measures taken to cut costs. About 90 percent of the organization's e-commerce sales are to North America and Europe.

"We have two dedicated salespeople in Toronto," Armstrong says. "From a sales perspective, NGOs take the units to countries where they practise and where there is a need. We have projects all over the world — Peru, Guatemala, Dominican Republic, Tanzania, Kenya, Senegal … and India is a huge one. We also distribute through our buy one, get one program, where we donate units for free and then we do an impact report on our website every year where we publish where those free units go. That program has had to evolve over the years, because it started off with the best intentions but was not executed properly."

Armstrong explains the execution issues arose because Lucky Iron Fish did not factor in distribution and training costs along with the uneven accounting impact on financials. The "buy one, give one" initiative required more complex accounting than expected and caused headaches and confusion on the organization's balance sheets for many years. The idea, while positive conceptually, was too complicated to implement, so the business eventually switched to an impact fund in 2022. Under this new structure a dedicated sum of money was used to donate units for free. While the concept of free units held plenty of merit, some of the firm's partners indicated they wanted a more holistic approach to iron deficiency that would involve matters such as diagnosing iron deficiency in communities, better educating individuals about the issue, and, as always, ever-evolving research.

"Also, there is a distribution cost, so if you are donating the units, you have to figure how to effectively get them out," Armstrong says. "So what we have landed on is we have actually turned our buy one, get one program into an impact fund that can be used to distribute free units, provide diagnostic equipment, run educational programs, or do research activities. NGOs have really valued that holistic approach to our impact."

Through that fund, Lucky Iron Fish donates to organizations in Canada, in the U.S., and around the world, such as food banks, Indigenous health care centres, and community-based organizations distributing food and aid baskets.

Currently there are eight full-time employees, two part-time employees, and a subcontracted employee. There are also five researchers who are paid by LIFe and work out of Carleton University in Ottawa, Ontario. By way of explanation, the Lucky Iron Fish name was altered to Lucky Iron Fish Enterprise (LIFe), which reflected the company's goals to scale into other innovations to tackle iron deficiency. Armstrong adds he sees the name as a clever marketing opportunity because *Fe* is the elemental symbol for iron. There's a finance person, a director of operations, an impact and partnerships director, a strategic partnerships director, an admin assistant, a digital marketing and brand director, and a customer service director. Manufacturing is outsourced, and the director of operations oversees that. The majority of the team is made up of women.

"We have done traditional hiring where when you've got a job, you post it, and do interviews, but then also I have found people that I really liked and asked them if they would like to work with us and created a role for them," Armstrong says. "Iron deficiency is primarily a women's health issue, so you typically find more energy and passion about it with women, so I wouldn't change a thing with our team. They're all fantastic."

Overall recent diversity and inclusion statistics for Lucky Iron Fish are as follows:

- 62% women
- 15% are living with a disability
- 23% are members of a visible minority
- 38% were born outside of Canada
- 31% have a first language other than English
- 31% are members of the 2SLGBTQIA+ community

As a startup, Lucky Iron Fish is on a revenue growth trajectory, but comparing revenue from a given month to the same month a year earlier does not always give the most accurate picture. Lucky Iron Fish received one large order in March 2019 that inflated the numbers a bit and makes March 2020 look like a decline by comparison. While the large order was welcome, the team is careful to explain the number comparison whenever needed.

Consumer education is an ongoing effort for Lucky Iron Fish, which has to be tailored to its two methods of moving the product. While it's the same product, it travels along two channels. They sell to NGOs in developing countries, and they sell directly to consumers around the world. With direct-to-consumer sales, the onus is on Lucky Iron Fish to educate people so they will want to purchase it.

That approach is done mainly through social media advertising and public relations.

"In developing countries, we work with NGO partners, designing education programs with them, thus it's basically a train-the-trainer model," Armstrong says. "In terms of embracing the education, it depends on the organization and their capacity. For example, we worked with World Vision in Tanzania. They purchased units for more than five thousand families, and we worked with them to design education and training materials in Swahili. We flew to Tanzania, met with the World Vision team, and trained the people who would be going into the communities and talking about [the Lucky Iron Fish]. We spent two days doing that training, and on the third day we actually went into a community for a sort of pilot and watched them do the presentation. One of the things we found very important was to do a cooking demonstration to show how to use it and show that it doesn't change the taste of the food. So we do a cooking demonstration, and we have people try the food, and when they realize it's okay, they are willing to use it."

Cultural sensitivity is always front of mind when working in developing countries, and Armstrong offers what he admits was a mistake to illustrate the point. When they developed their educational materials in Swahili, it turned out the translator was from Kenya and not Tanzania, so they had been translated into a different dialect.

"We just incorrectly assumed that Swahili was Swahili," he says.

As for building relations with NGOs, in some cases they come to Lucky Iron Fish because they hear about the product from advertising, from public relations, or at conferences, such as at international nutritional conferences. Alternately, Armstrong and his team will approach them, knowing where the big NGOs are, in particular those working with iron deficiency specifically.

"Sometimes we have a corporate partner," Armstrong explains. "So Burberry, for example, through the Burberry Foundation, purchased units for cotton farmers. Obviously, they don't market health products, so we formed a collaboration with an NGO in Peru that focuses on newborn and youth nutrition and health to actually do education and distribution. We went to the NGO and said, 'We have some funds from a private organization; what would it take to have you distribute these units?'"

Armstrong credits the Guelph area's Quentin Johnson, a world-renowned expert in food fortification and iron fortification, for pointing him in the direction of electrolytic iron. Johnson has an honorary degree from the University of Guelph, and he knew about Lucky Iron Fish's work after meeting Armstrong at several university events.

"At a conference, he came across a company called IMP, Industrial Metal Powders," Armstrong says. IMP was based in India. "IMP made food-grade electrical iron powder, which is used in food fortification, and he made the connection that it could be possible to make the fish out of that. He connected us over email, and we had some great phone calls. We actually ended up flying to India to meet with them to understand if they could make the fish for us. They had really great quality-control capabilities on site. They had a lab. Something that was just very nice was that they are a family-run business. You could just tell they cared about our mission. We would not be their largest customer, because they work with international food companies. But they really believed in our work. They cooked us lunch and we ate with them. They wanted to really build a relationship. They planted a tree in their garden in our honour. As the relationship grows, the tree will grow. So that is where the fish are all made today."

As the relationship was developing and as more trials were conducted, it was emerging that the electrolytic iron fish were more effective, with a higher bioavailability rate, meaning the proportion of a nutrient that enters the circulation in the body is able to have an active effect. During the transition to electrolytic fish, some of the clinical trials were still using the cast-iron versions, Armstrong says. Lucky Iron Fish failed to distinguish between the two kinds of fish, and as a result, some of the data were mixed up. This made the transition take longer, but eventually the switch was made.

In the course of the growth of Lucky Iron Fish, due to a number of factors — his tenacity, vision, commitment — Armstrong has developed a strong group of admirers. Among them is Lang, dating to his days at Guelph's business school and when she served as the director of the Centre for Business and Student Enterprise.

"The entrepreneurial journey, or the struggle that entrepreneurs go through, is that when they're in the middle of something, they're wearing all the hats," she says. "So they're the marketer, they're the designer, they're the accountant, the lawyer, the salesperson. When you're in the business, you don't take time to celebrate your milestones and recognize your achievements, you just move on to the next thing. So I think it's so important, when you are doing the work that Gavin has done over the years, to take stock and pause and recognize the milestones, because that further fuels you going forward."

Another person who has a lot of time and respect for Armstrong is Kate Stevenson. Her connection with Armstrong dates to their days serving on the University of Guelph's board of directors. The Harvard graduate worked on Wall Street, is a corporate director for a number of organizations, and did time with firms such as Nortel.

"I think that one of the things that I enjoy most is learning about people, recognizing talent, surrounding myself with good people, usually smarter than myself," she says. "It was at first a working relationship that grew into a friendship. I feel that I am a friend of Lucky Iron Fish. I'm a friend of Gavin's and certainly passionate about what he is trying to achieve."

With so much of her career spent in corporate settings, she describes Lucky Iron Fish as being on the opposite end of the spectrum, the opposite of big capitalist enterprises.

"It was the antithesis of everything I had learned to navigate, and in some ways, I tried to master it because of it being a social enterprise. In the early startup days, I often thought to myself, 'What could I offer?' Often late at night, Gavin would call and say, 'What about this? Or how might you organize this group, or this human resources issue?' We just had lots of back and forth, and I just loved watching his company grow. It's really a great joy to be able to talk with him and navigate some of the challenges that he has."

Another admirer of Lucky Iron Fish and Armstrong is the previously introduced Whitfield, who connected with him when they were both undergrads at the University of Guelph, and continued the connection when they were graduate students, she at the University of British Columbia and he at Guelph. At one point it turned out they were both doing research in Cambodia at the same time.

Whitfield, from Belleville, Ontario, was studying nutrition, in particular a micronutrient deficiency disorder that is most prevalent in Cambodia: vitamin B1 deficiency. She used to live there half-time and still has an active research program there.

"I think [the reason] Gavin has had such great professional success is that people like to spend time with him."

Jenn Souter describes herself as a friend and cheerleader for Lucky Iron Fish and Armstrong, too.

"I just think that what he does is so amazing, so cool — my coolest friend," she says. "I actually, a long time ago, bought one for myself. My wife has issues — she's immune-compromised and has very low iron. So we use it all the time. The impression I get is that social awareness and social activism is a really important component in Gavin's life, and that Lucky Iron Fish and what he is doing with the organization really plays into that.

"I think one of the most impressive things was when they took the Lucky Iron Fish and turned it into a leaf, because they realized that it was more appealing in communities with a vegetarian culture. That revealed cultural awareness, to shift the product to account for that."

The leaf design was named the Lucky Iron Leaf, but in India Gavin decided to name it the Lucky Shakti Leaf. *Shakti* means "power" in Hindi and has been used for names in other iron fortification programs.

Schuurman of the CGLCC adds observations from a business perspective. "If he can be successful as a business and influence change, that's a pretty valuable combination. It's something that we're seeing — people are starting to realize that the two don't have to be mutually exclusive. You can be a large corporation or a mid-sized company while still looking to do good, and consumers are more and more demanding of that now. So it's about social responsibility."

# Chapter 6

# Scoring in the *Dragons' Den*

WHILE PLANNING, RESEARCH, and determination are essential for an idea — in this case, a business — to take off or expand, sometimes other events can help propel its success. Some are unexpected, such as the BBC mentioning Lucky Iron Fish, leading to a surge in interest. Others are pursued deliberately, as in the case of Armstrong's 2018 appearance on the CBC's *Dragons' Den*, a popular TV show based on the internationally franchised *Dragons' Den* format, which began in Japan. Budding Canadian entrepreneurs pitch business and investment ideas to a panel of venture capitalists (called "Dragons") with the goal of securing business financing and partnerships. At the time, the show was drawing a weekly audience of about nine hundred thousand viewers.

The show had long been on Armstrong's radar.

"I was a fan of *Dragons' Den* for years, as someone who's always been interested in entrepreneurship. Shows like that always excited me," he says. "I loved seeing the ideas and the pitches, and I dreamed about being on it one day. Lucky Iron Fish had already raised money, just over a million dollars of investment, before I went on *Dragons' Den*. As a result, I had become pretty good at pitches. I worked on pitching through a lot of pitch workshops and mentoring practices and competitions. I like the Q&A part because it's more engaging, more of a dialogue."

Interestingly, despite his fondness for the show and earlier dreams of being on it someday, it was *Dragons' Den* producers who reached out to Lucky Iron Fish and invited Armstrong to audition for the show, saying that they felt the product was a great fit — and Armstrong didn't want to do it.

Armstrong says that given all his experience with and knowledge about raising money, he was not particularly impressed by the deals he saw being made on the show, pointing out a common example of an entrepreneur turning over 50 percent of their company for a two-hundred-thousand-dollar investment.

"I did not want terms like that," he says, though he knew the oral agreements made during the show are not binding.

By that point, he had raised money, had gained valuation experience, and was secure in knowing what he wanted. "I didn't want to give away the company just to be on a reality TV show."

Armstrong actually turned down *Dragons' Den* auditions twice, and in the meantime, he went on another reality show called *Boss Swap*, where participants would run each other's company for a day. After the show, while debriefing with the CEO he'd swapped with, that CEO asked Armstrong if he had ever been on *Dragons' Den*. Armstrong said he hadn't, explaining that the deals he had seen on the show were not what he was seeking.

"Then she said, 'Well, I've been on *Dragons' Den*, and those deals are just kind of for TV. There's a lot of negotiating that happens after the show. And it's not like a verbal agreement is going to bind you. But it's amazing publicity, one of the best PR opportunities you can have. You should do it.'"

So when *Dragons' Den* reached out again, Armstrong gave the green light, having listened to the other CEO and weighed her recommendation. He was anxious get on with it.

"I still had to go through the audition process, where they ask you questions about your business and probe some inner details of what you'd be looking for," he notes. "It's more along the lines of looking under the hood."

With the commitment to the show in place, he moved into preparation mode. Armstrong would later preach what he had practised, penning a blog post about how to succeed on *Dragons' Den*.

A key stage in preparing was making sure to do his homework. Armstrong said he watched numerous previous episodes to learn what to do and what not to do. He studied the kinds of questions that were asked of participants and what responses were successful. He studied how the entrepreneurs presented themselves.

"I watched multiple episodes a day. I wrote down the most common questions they asked, and I created a cheat sheet for myself that I just constantly memorized. When I watched the shows and the Dragons would ask a question, I would answer with my own answer. I practised by watching the shows and doing practice pitches to the virtual Dragons."

In another recommendation from his blog post, he drives home the point that it is a marathon, not a sprint.

"When I watched previous episodes, I was always stunned that an investment decision could be made in under ten minutes," he says. "It turns out that that is not true. My actual pitch to the Dragons was just under an hour long, but it was edited down to eight minutes and thirty seconds. You need to be prepared to stand and speak for a long time."

Through his pre-taping research, he picked up patterns in the Dragons' questions, noticing they often asked similar questions about the business's valuation or what will be done with investments or projected cash flows.

"So I felt really prepared," he recalls. "This is a bit superficial, but I picked out this flashy outfit, because I wanted to stand out and look like I was in control. But in the morning when I was getting ready, I got nervous, and I didn't want to wear that outfit. So I just put on a blazer and a dress shirt. It wasn't that I thought they would make fun of me for my outfit, I just felt like I needed to be in comfortable, relaxed, conservative clothing."

Another step in preparing was identifying the tools and props that could be used to enliven the pitch. In particular in Armstrong's case, he and team member Anne Pringle put together a tray with prepared iron lemonade for the Dragons.

"It was pre-made because it takes ten minutes to boil, and I didn't want to stand there for ten minutes waiting," he recalls.

"I remember the day quite well," he continues. "They give you a date to show up at the studio in Toronto, and they tell you your filming time will be between early morning and early evening, but you have no idea when you're going to go. And you're just nervous."

It was an intimidating experience, being in a huge studio surrounded by other entrepreneurs trying to get deals. Pringle joined Armstrong at the studio to keep him company and practise with him. But he had to go out and pitch alone.

"Anne just tried her best to distract me, so we were laughing and talking about things, but every once in a while, I would read my cheat sheet again and the nerves would resurface," he recalls.

While he waited, the producers wanted Armstrong to film a promotional piece for the show.

"They just wanted me to say something like 'there's nothing fishy about this deal,'" he says. "I was so nervous that I was coming across like a robot, and they were saying loosen up, loosen up, count to ten, shake your arms. But every time I did it I just came across as scared. I knew that at any moment they were going to call my name for my turn at the show."

Armstrong says they had him do the take ten to fifteen times, and in the end, they never used the clip.

"So then, my next biggest fear was that I was going to screw up and become like an internet meme — you see all these *Dragons' Den* fails on the internet where people are just mocked or do something stupid or say something stupid. And I was afraid that that was going to be me," he says. "I just had this fear of really embarrassing myself.

"When your number is up, you go out and you have to walk down the stairs and they film you as you do this. The Dragons are already sitting there, and you're not supposed to start until they say go. Okay, so you just stand there and you're staring at the Dragons and they're staring back at you. And it's just silence. It was so intimidating.

"I think one of them was on their phone and they're talking to each other, so they're not trying to intimidate you, but you just want to start. Then they said go and I counted down in my head from three to one. And then I did my thing. I'm in the present. It was the same way that I am with presentations. I'm very nervous leading up to it, but once I'm on stage, I'm good. It's a sort of performance thing, where I'll be nervous and afraid, but then the minute I get on stage, I get this burst of energy. And I'm like that now with investment pitches or speeches or anything. Once the spotlight is on, it's like a different personality takes over.

"So they said go and I started the pitch. And I'm doing, I think, a pretty good job, everything's working. And we had the tray with all the lemonade, as well as samples of the fish on it. And I had to pick up the tray and walk it over to them and give them the glasses. The tray was kind of heavy and I kept thinking, 'Oh my god, if you trip and fall, you're going to spill drinks on one of these Gucci designer outfits.' And that would have been the *Dragons' Den* fail that was going to be the internet sensation that you'll be remembered for. The tray was shaking when I walked."

But he managed to deliver the lemonade incident-free, no Gucci was harmed, and it was time to move on to the Q&A, which is when Armstrong says he always gets his mojo back. "I enjoy conversation and discussion and I can explain things in a bit more detail."

In the close to one hour of exchange, there is a lot of give-and-take that gets trimmed to get the episode down to just over eight minutes.

"There were a lot more questions that were very business-specific that I think wouldn't really be interesting to viewers," Armstrong explains, crediting the editors for trimming the piece while keeping it meaningful.

He says the conversation was a good exchange packed with solid questions, and as it evolved the Dragons were very complimentary, which left him convinced he had pulled off the presentation.

"Once they started saying positive things, I remember thinking I had won, because even if they don't offer you a deal, you got the PR, and they said nice things about the concept," he says. "I thought the best takeaway at that moment was that they loved the product. Even if they had said they loved it, 'but it's just not right for us and we wish you luck,' I was good with that."

But as the show went on, the Dragons and Armstrong began talking deals.

"Some of the Dragons said, 'You know, I love what you're doing but I think the others would be a better fit for you, so I'm not going to offer but I wish you luck.' So then it became Arlene Dickinson, Michele Romanow, and Manjit Minhas who were offering investments, and I actually tried to negotiate with them," Armstrong continues. "Arlene was saying, 'I can help you with the NGO world,' and Michele was saying, 'I know e-commerce,' and Manjit was saying, 'I know India and have lots of connections in India,' which is where we had really put our focus up to Covid-19.

"I was thinking, 'Well, these are the three things I need help with, why don't I have them all come in together.' So that's when I asked if the three of them would combine their offers. Michele and

Manjit said yes. Arlene said no, that she really wanted to do it on her own."

Armstrong said he had a moment of panic at that point in trying to consider how to move forward, and even considered asking for five minutes to consider the situation quietly.

"I kind of was a little panicky, but I thought, 'Well, India and e-commerce are two of the check boxes,' so I opted to go with the two even though I really respect Arlene a lot," he recalls. "Arlene said the things she said — I think she was a little bit pissed off."

And then it was over and Armstrong walked off the set. There was some post-production activity where they filmed Armstrong to get his reactions. He apologized for having been nervous in the taping, but they assured him that he seemed fine and had done a great job.

"And then I talked to Anne and gave her a big hug," he says. Anne had been unable to be in the studio for the taping, so she had no idea how it had gone. "I was going to try to hide it from her and be cool, but I couldn't. I was just so happy," he admits. They contacted other team members to share the good news. But they were all required to remain quiet about the show until it aired, which was on September 18, 2018.

"One thing I recall is that when you're waiting to go up and film, there are big doors that people come in and out of, and you know, people go in, they're nervous, they're excited, and some people come out and they're so happy," Armstrong says. "And some people come out and they just have this defeated look on their face. It's actually upsetting. I came out and I was so happy. I was smiling and jumping. But the group that came out right before me was taking down their booth. And you could see tears in their eyes. So I just determined that I didn't want to display my happiness around someone who obviously didn't have a good experience," he says, and he adjusted his behaviour so that he wouldn't be too conspicuous with his excitement.

Armstrong was contacted separately by Michele and Manjit and their teams, and the due diligence began, at which point Armstrong was in a position to share details such as financials.

"The reality is that post–due diligence, and once you get into the realities of investing, the deal structures are often different from what's talked about on TV," he says.

It was during this period that the young entrepreneur received a call with a pleasant surprise. "It was one of our due diligence calls with Manjit," Armstrong remembers. "She said, 'Just so you know, the Dragons pick their favourite pitches, and they go on the season premiere — and yours is one of them, so you're going to be on episode one of the new season.'"

Armstrong was blown away by the news and started putting a plan in place to celebrate the season opener. A party was planned at the Lucky Iron Fish office with staff, board members, and friends and family, supplied with plenty of wine and food.

"We watched the episode live. I hadn't seen the edit, so I didn't know how or what they were going to show," he says. "I was seeing it for the first time, and it was great. You're obviously pumped, and all the people cheered, and it was lovely."

The impact of the *Dragons' Den* appearance was overwhelming. In the first twenty-four hours after the prime-time debut, online sales jumped more than 500 percent, and the business received increased traffic over the following weekend. They see similar bumps every time the episode airs as a rerun.

"I'm still recognized to this day for being on *Dragons' Den*," he says. "I went to the bank to get currency exchanged and the guy said, 'I recognize you from somewhere. I think I saw you on *Dragons' Den*.' People have recognized me at parties. I get people who message me on Instagram: 'Hey, I just saw your episode. I love what you're doing, can I ask you questions?' And the thing about *Dragons' Den* that's great is it's on Netflix. It's on VIA Rail. It's on

Air Canada. Even now, when we go to conferences or trade shows, and we're talking about Lucky Iron Fish, the number of people who still say, 'Oh, I saw that on *Dragons' Den*' is incredible."

Armstrong acknowledges that it was fortunate the show aired before the pandemic, so when it hit he was in position to benefit from Michele Romanow's expertise in e-commerce. "Michele is an active investor and always willing to help."

Other than a subsequent survey there was little follow up from the show, though he adds if there were an opportunity to participate again he would jump at the chance.

Armstrong has a few takeaways from the *Dragons' Den* experience.

"For one, an entrepreneur doesn't necessarily have to have every single skill set to start a business. That's why partnerships can be really important, as are strong teams. When you watch *Dragons' Den*, you realize there are some good ideas that don't have the best ambassadors.

"And pitching is hard, it's a certain skill set that not everyone has. I used to have a fear of public speaking. I used to shake. But at Guelph, Alastair [Summerlee] helped me, and he basically said, 'Okay, you're going to give the convocation address and speak in front of two thousand people. You have to practise every day.' I was mortified but I did it.

"Then I just kept volunteering and doing more and more public speaking activities, to the point where I spoke in a stadium with Bill Clinton in front of thousands of people. So now I have the ability to do these things.

"If you're someone who just doesn't have that and you're more of the behind-the-scenes person, you have to have a partner who can be the ambassador, because pitching is critical. You are the face of your business. If you're not comfortable in that position, fine, but you must find someone who is."

# Chapter 7

# Coping Through the Pandemic

ARMSTRONG FACED A new and unique challenge when he found himself cornered on the other side of the world with two of his team members as the Covid-19 crisis exploded globally in March 2020. He and two staff members had just arrived. They were brimming with optimism over the future of Lucky Iron Fish. *Dragons' Den* had delivered a huge boost. Significant events were on tap for the trip. There were meetings planned with government representatives, both Canadian and Indian, important discussions were on the books with key manufacturers, and social events were slated, designed to spread the Lucky Iron Fish story. Then came Covid-19.

As shared earlier, Armstrong had faced down a range of challenges growing up, from bullying to coming to terms with his sexuality. With all those years of handling such issues under his belt, Armstrong had dealt with enough stormy seas to be prepared to confront the Covid-19 curveball in India. There was a tremendous emotional element to the challenge, of course. The Lucky Iron Fish could aid as many as two billion people around the planet, mainly women and children, who suffer from iron deficiency. The Covid-19 setback meant the lofty plans to enhance the manufacturing and distribution of the health-giving product would be seriously slowed.

"Every day, it seemed like the situation got worse," Armstrong explains. "Because of the time-zone differences, it felt like you woke up to a new world every day. And it was becoming clearer and clearer how serious things were getting.

"I'd wake up to developments that had happened in Canada, and then it would be silent because it would be nighttime there," he recalled. "You would wake up — and our hotel was pretty empty because people weren't travelling — and you sort of felt disconnected from the rest of the world. You would go online and see the massive lineups at grocery stores, people fighting over toilet paper, and there I am at breakfast and it's peaceful and quiet. You're feeling isolated from the challenges, but you knew that they were real, and you had to accept them."

As those circumstances worsened before his eyes, Armstrong admits that he was frantically trying to find ways to push through with the visit, looking back now and recognizing that he may have allowed himself a sense of denial of the harsh reality all around him.

"So much was riding on the success of the India expansion," he says. "We had — I don't know precisely how much money — tens of thousands invested in this initiative. For the investors themselves, we were promising deliverables. We had clinical trials that had been going on for years, at least two to three years of work that was being discussed and disseminated. And the trajectory for the next year was built on the sales in India, the growth in India."

This was a daily drama faced by Armstrong and his team members, bolstered by the persistent worry that the bold India initiative was going to fall through, and it was "terrifying. I was trying to salvage as much as I could of the trip."

Armstrong had met with government officials in Mumbai, and the encounter offered a reason for much hope, a brighter reality on the horizon. But then he learned that two more team members, who had been about to leave Canada to join the team in India, were denied entry to the South Asian country. The gravest of concerns had become a harsh reality.

"I was still trying to salvage what I could, see if we could walk away with one deal or just get something to happen. My judgment was clouded by that. Then when things got shut down in Mumbai, I went to New Delhi, and even there, because the situation felt different, we said we were going to try to accomplish a couple of things. We were very secluded; we were in a hotel compound. Mumbai has way more people on top of each other than Delhi."

Nevertheless, a long series of questions was constantly front of mind for Armstrong. Could they see anyone in Delhi to try to nail down at least some accomplishments? Would it be difficult to get back to Canada? Would it even be possible for the three of them to go back together? How bad was the situation becoming in Canada? And, really, in all those challenges, the outcomes were pretty much out of his control.

Recognition of the lack of control at that time draws a smile from Armstrong. "I can laugh now because that is the feedback that I always get: It's that I am only comfortable when I'm in full control. Even when I don't want to be in control, I'm still in control."

So at the core of his desire to salvage any accomplishment was his need to identify anything over which there could be some control.

"I just tried to focus on what I could control, and that included trying to get meetings out of it. So instead of doing a major event, we identified who the five people that we really wanted to meet with were and tried to set up individual, quick meetings. They could come to the hotel, or we would go to their office. We took hotel vehicles that felt more sanitized. We were trying to salvage what we could. Focusing on what I could control maybe also meant that I was not paying the attention I should have been to what was happening back home."

Armstrong notes that having two colleagues along proved beneficial, not least for the emotional support.

"We were able to debrief regularly and go over what we were hearing about what was happening back home," he says. "The way the time zones work, I felt like I went to bed every night right after Prime Minister Justin Trudeau did his morning press conference. Every morning, he would address the issue, and for me that was about eleven at night. We were able to get a snapshot of what the day looked like in Canada."

"Yeah, it was harrowing," explains Anne Pringle, one of two team members with Armstrong in India. "Hindsight is 20/20, and maybe we should have known more. But when my colleague Shraddha [Sekhon] and I flew over, Gavin was already in India. When we were in the air — I think it takes fifteen hours or so to fly from Toronto to Delhi — a lot changed. One thing was that the Indian government decided during the night that after the next forty-eight hours, they would stop accepting foreign visas and tourists or people on business coming in. And then over the next day or two, that's when it was declared a global pandemic and borders started getting shut down. But India was not shutting down the way Canada was, so it felt like weird parallel universes."

The minute team members Stephanie Bergeron and Angela McMonagle were denied their flight to India and barred from entering the country, they all knew that was a sign of things to come, Armstrong says.

"The fear became really obvious. It's a public health issue," he says. "At that time, there really wasn't clear messaging about how it spread, and how infectious it was. The default is always, well, let's assume the worst and then scale it back, because you'd rather overestimate than underestimate. And you're in India so there's no space and you're just constantly around people. At least some measures were being put in place, such as at the airport, where they were doing temperature checks. But the lineup was back-to-back, so there was no social distancing. You do start to feel anxious, and you wonder about the importance of wearing masks and if they prevent infection, because at that point, I think people thought wearing a mask would prevent you from catching it, not from spreading it. It was the other way around.

"When we were in the car going to meetings, we were hand sanitizing like crazy and we felt constantly anxious. Shraddha, every time she goes to India, she buys spices to bring home with her. We went to this market, and it instantly felt unsafe; there were so many people. And by this point, we had made a decision we were going home. And I actually just said, 'I don't feel comfortable doing this. I don't think this is a good idea.' And we just turned around and went back to the hotel."

The excitement from the ambitious plans for the India foray only intensified the disappointment.

"We were actually organizing one of the largest endeavours that we as a company had ever done," Armstrong explains. "The plan was to host two research dissemination meetings, one in Mumbai and one in New Delhi, to talk about all of the research findings that we had from our clinical trials. We were going to host panels on the role of innovation in solving iron deficiency and we were going to highlight some case studies of what we had done in the past and how we had worked with the private sector and the civil society sector. For New Delhi, it was going to be hosted at the high commissioner's official residence, and the high commissioner was going to open the event. We had high-level panellists participating. In Mumbai the Canadian counsel general was going to open it. We had spent months organizing it, we had spent a lot of money, and then it all unravelled over the course of three or four days."

Another initiative that had to be scratched — another source of disappointment — was the plan to announce the opening of a LIFe office in India.

When the trio made the decision to cancel the Delhi event, they firmed up the decision to get back to Canada. Making that decision was one thing, but arranging a flight was another and it was going to take a couple of days to get on one.

"So we said, 'Well, we're here, we might as well try to pack in meetings these days.'" Armstrong recalls. "It wasn't like we left it to the last minute and then just went to the airport. We got the earliest flight we could, but that was still two or three days away, so we just said, 'Okay, we've got a couple of days here, let's try to connect.' We only did four meetings. But we did them."

"We each had plans to keep travelling," says Armstrong. "Anne was going on a vacation with her partner after India. He was flying to meet her and they were going to go to Sri Lanka. And I was actually going to Bangkok and then the U.K. because I was going to the Micronutrient Forum and the Skoll World Forum [which explores entrepreneurial solutions to global issues], and that is a really big deal. It's an invitation-only event, so I was really looking forward to that. It eventually went virtual. And we were just all wondering, what's going to happen without the India trip and the money that was invested in that. There was all this stress.

"There were immediate concerns and it looked like the world was collapsing around us. We didn't know how long lockdowns were going to last. I was wondering if I should go back to Canada and then go to the U.K., and what was happening with this trip and that trip. I don't think at the time we thought this was going to be a multi-year thing. There was so much unknown and uncertainty about everything."

Despite being in the same circumstance as them, Armstrong felt responsibility for Anne and Shraddha.

"I think I feel that way all the time, no matter what's going on, and it means putting on a brave face. I was trying not to let my anxiety or fear come through while listening to how they were feeling. And we talked about what was going on all the time. But because we were so far removed, I don't know if they were as stressed as I was. I felt like parts of Lucky Iron Fish were collapsing. And I had to worry about the safety of two team members who were with me. There was an uncertainty around what was happening with my family back home. I just felt like I was carrying all this added weight on me."

Shraddha and Anne also expressed their anxiety.

"I don't think they really knew how bad it was until we got back to Canada," Armstrong says. "I was booking the flights and there was still this sort of reservation of, well, why didn't I just go home and the others could continue, because Anne wanted to go on her vacation and Shraddha was going to see her family. Then at one point, I did say, 'No, you're on a company trip, I'm responsible for you. You're coming home.'"

Once the trio was at the airport, they learned Sri Lanka had closed its borders, and later there was news about people who were stuck in India for months.

"I don't think anyone would say I made the wrong decision," Armstrong says. "It was just a shitty decision. We had to cancel Anne's vacation. No one likes that, of course, but it was the right thing to do."

"It speaks to his character, as well, because he had two colleagues with him," explains friend Lachowsky. "And he wanted to do everything in his power to make sure that they could stay together to come back. And all that did was probably quadruple the challenge of pulling it off."

Lachowsky and Armstrong have had several international travel experiences together, such as to Ecuador.

"You end up in situations and I think you learn how to survive in some of those different environments," Lachowsky says. "And when you're confronted by different kinds of threats or challenges, [you learn] the value of sticking together. I mean, if nothing else, at least you have each other and you know each other. It's a kind of trust and comfort where even if you worry about wellness, you have that mental assuredness. It's important.

"And then I think the other piece is just responsibility for each other. I mean, Gavin was very aware of what that journey meant, but he had responsibility for the people with him."

Ultimately, Armstrong did manage to secure three tickets back to Canada for the three of them on the same flight.

"I had been trying to find a flight where the three of us could be together," he says. "I didn't want everyone to have to go on their own, but because the flight restrictions were coming into effect, a lot of the flights were through China, which we couldn't do, so I eventually found the three last tickets on a flight to Toronto via Dubai, so we just packed up and left, and finally it was a little stressful. When you're calling Air Canada, you're on hold for ages, but I would say Air Canada did a great job in trying to help us."

Armstrong's mother, Linda, says she was not surprised by his concern for his team members.

"He's very good with all his employees and always compassionate with them," she says. "Even while we were in Covid-19 and working at home, we'd have daily meetings, so we were all motivated every day. He's a very good manager and business leader."

Despite the success in securing three tickets to Canada, the disappointment over how the India trip had been severely limited was palpable. What-ifs abounded. Questions about how to move forward were unending and they were going to have to be answered in an environment for which there was no real playbook: a pandemic.

Still, in the face of dismay, Armstrong opted to make the most of their departure from India.

"Something that I did that I was really proud of is I spent the flight from Dubai to Toronto, many hours, doing two things," he recalls. "I wrote a strategic plan outlining how I thought the pandemic could impact the company and the steps we needed to take to mitigate that. And I wrote a staff email saying here's the concern, here's what we know, and here's what steps we're going to take. Later I got feedback from board members saying they sat on big corporate boards, and it took weeks for them to get the kind of document that they got from me the day we landed. I knew it was going to be an issue, so I decided we had to figure out what to do and start planning for the worst-case scenarios.

"I had so much confidence in how we were going to handle this problem. But I think the combination of the stress of the pandemic, the toll of being alone, the toll of being isolated, the work, still recovering from the trip, and I was going through a breakup — I was paying a heavy price. Then I had a call with a board member who basically said the worst-case scenario is going to happen, so let's start planning for shutting down and just closing up. And for the first time in years, I hung up the phone and I just cried for an hour. Everything came out."

# Chapter 8

# The Future of LIFe

WHILE THOSE TEARS may have been understandable at the time, they did not foreshadow what was to come. Much of the ensuing months involved implementing the plans Armstrong had set out on the flight to Canada from India, and those plans were essential to surviving and even thriving through the bleaker moments of the pandemic.

A sign that his plan to ride out the pandemic was solid is the fact that staffing levels remained essentially the same throughout.

"We did use the government programs that were available, because we did see a decline in revenue," he says. "I did everything I could to protect staff. We did have to let one staff person go, because they weren't able to do their job in international sales because of the pandemic. We couldn't go internationally, so we just couldn't sustain that position. They understood. I mean, it was an emotional time, but they understood."

Another step in sustaining the business's viability was cost cutting.

"It was a matter of just looking at your costs, and staff salaries are the number one cost that you don't want to touch," he explains. "It means looking at what else you can trim to minimize your cash burn, so that you don't have to resort to laying off staff. We got rid of our office space and obviously we weren't travelling. We just looked at efficiencies and ways to reduce our cash burden, our expense burden."

Armstrong acknowledges that the business was in the fortuitous position of having already established a solid foothold in its e-commerce sales stream.

"I think everyone in the world thought e-commerce would suffer, but e-commerce boomed," he points out. "And so we were able to ride that wave like other businesses were, and it was that cash that helped us survive. If we hadn't been equipped to do e-commerce, or we had been late to the game, I don't think we would have been as successful as we were, but we already had an established strategy."

While e-commerce provided a strong lifeline for the business, there were still significant challenges to address. One was managing the supply chain, the result of what Armstrong describes as a "perfect storm." Thanks to the e-commerce success, sales were significantly outpacing the Lucky Iron Fish team's projections.

"But there were shutdowns in India, which meant they couldn't produce units," he explains. "And there were shipping backlogs because of all the shutdowns. Then when we finally had units produced, they took forever to get here to Canada. For the first time in the company's life, we were out of stock. That meant we couldn't sell on Amazon because you can't sell unless you have product in the warehouse. Half of our sales come from Amazon. So then we had to do back orders from our website."

Eventually the backlogs in India opened up and production began to normalize again. In the end they were out of stock for more than a month, and it was a costly pause.

"That was a lot of money, something in the range of fifty thousand bucks a week," he estimates.

"It was a long pandemic. In 2020 there was uncertainty, a reduction in revenue. Then 2021, leading into 2022, was when the e-commerce boom grew," he says, adding, ironically, "the company actually saw its first profitable quarters after ten years of its life. It was during the pandemic that we actually started to edge close to profitability."

Guelph's Moreton points to how the company met the challenges of the pandemic as a measure of the business's future.

"I would say the most significant and telling thing about the success of the business is that they survived the pandemic," he says. "And that is a feat, I think, in itself, because they had to manage, for example, manufacturing from halfway around the world and the supply chain in general, and all of that was well-handled."

With the strong foothold delivered by e-commerce coupled with the winding down of the pandemic, the Lucky Iron Fish team is able to look to the future with optimism and confidence.

"I think that for the business to survive and thrive, we need to grow," Armstrong explains. "Our flagship product, the Lucky Iron Fish, has been really successful in helping people by having a global impact and establishing our brand. But it's not enough to take us to where we want to go. I want us to be a business that is a leader in all things iron deficiency."

In that vein, as this story was being written, the business was transitioning to a new brand name, Lucky Iron Life. "[The new name] is meant to encompass the fact that we now are providing a multitude of solutions to address the global problem of iron deficiency," Armstrong says. "The focus is going to be on simple solutions to diagnose and treat iron deficiency in the short term. For instance, we've developed an iron-enriched powder that can be used in everyday cooking. And it can be used in large volume cooking for NGOs."

He points to the example of NGOs operating in India, which Armstrong would meet with regularly. They prepare midday-meal programs that involve cooking food in huge industrial kitchens using industrial-size pots. "It's the largest midday-meal program in the world," he says. "One hundred and thirty million kids are fed lunch every single day. If we can get into half a percent of that market, we're doing a pretty good job.

"There will be the NGO application, but there is also going to be a consumer angle," Armstrong continues. "For example, you can buy the powder for yourself and put it on your food in the morning or in your smoothie, similar to other kinds of nutrient powder."

Clinical testing of the powder was completed in early 2023.

Armstrong says there are other ideas in the works for becoming the go-to brand for addressing iron deficiency. One product could be for women who are menstruating, a segment of the population often susceptible to iron deficiency. Examples of such products could be iron-rich chocolate bars or iron-rich tea. "We're exploring potential products that can help alleviate some of the discomforts around menstruation, while also providing the necessary iron," he explains.

"We're looking at very specific branded products for target demographics who are at risk of iron deficiency and need more iron — populations such as vegans, vegetarians, athletes, pregnant women, or women trying to get pregnant. I would like to have targeted solutions for all of those at-risk demographics."

As for the India NGO initiatives, Armstrong notes that the team is working with some of the largest organizations operating there. He describes his visits to the NGOs as hitting the ground running.

"In one case I started pretty much right away," he recalls. "I was driven to a production kitchen for one of those midday-meal programs. To get there you have to leave at three in the morning. I was given a tour of the kitchen, then I met with their nutrition team and their procurement team to talk about the data regarding iron deficiency. I needed to understand what their needs were and how our powder could be beneficial. And then I just tried to learn about the system and figure out what we would need to do to make sure the powder is meeting their needs in the quantities they would require."

Again, with an eye to the future, Lucky Iron Fish's team of five researchers worked on developing the iron powder and will be instrumental in helping to explore new products. Armstrong has been able to retain the Ottawa-based group thanks to funding the company received for research innovation.

"And so those researchers, in part, are being paid for by grants from the Government of Canada, which is very helpful," he says.

In developing the iron fish and powder themselves, and any other potential future products, Armstrong notes that there are always "technical, nitty-gritty questions to deal with." He points to the powder as an example.

"We were at a unique point where the powder itself had been developed, but we didn't have any of the specifics around, for example, its packaging," he says. "You're asking the NGO what type of package it should come in, or if a bucket would be better than a bag. There are questions with respect to what your dream product would be, or how it would be delivered and at what frequency. Then we are able to build the execution of the product based on feedback from the NGOs.

"Like everything we do, I want to make sure that it has a sustainability element to it," he adds. "They'll tell us how they want the product to come, but then we will look at ways to make sure it still meets our threshold for sustainable systems, minimal packaging, printing, reducing our footprint, things like that."

For Armstrong and the Lucky Iron Fish team, packaging is an ongoing concern. "One of the pieces of advice we got when entering India, and something we heard from multiple people, is that you want to find ways to have the most amount of recurring revenue," he says, pointing to examples of haircare companies that, instead of selling bottles of shampoo, sell daily packets because they are quicker to produce and cost less, but consumers end up buying more of them so the companies make more money over the long run.

"And these people said we should do that," Armstrong continues. "But I don't want to have a daily piece of plastic that you throw out in the garbage, because that for me does not make any type of environmental sense. I put my foot down and said, 'I'm not even going to entertain this idea.' I will not sacrifice our impact objectives for an extra couple bucks. I'm not going to make more money by hurting the planet at the same time."

With this range of initiatives factoring into longer term plans, Armstrong anticipates changes in operational and sales roles.

"I see us building out the sales team, the marketing team, and then the operational support to assist with that," he adds. "We definitely would bring in experts to lead research initiatives, but the problem is that we're held to a different standard when it comes to conflict of interest. We learned that with the iron fish — we did our own clinical trials, and I was a student, but I still got the criticism: you're commercializing this, you're going to make money from it, so your research is invalid.

"We took those lessons for the powder. And that's why Carleton University in Ottawa is doing the clinical trials for us. I don't know if we'd ever bring research in-house, just because there's that concern or that perception about conflict of interest. It's frustrating, because pharma companies do their own research, and I don't see anyone not using their vaccines or buying their pills. But we're not big pharma, so I think it would be safer and meet ethical standards for us to continue to outsource research for the next five years at least."

And while there is significant need in lower-income countries around the world, demand for iron support is universal.

"I think iron deficiency itself doesn't discriminate, it's just more common among certain populations," Armstrong explains. "And one of those populations is low-income communities, especially women in low-income communities. But I do think there is a lot of symmetry in the sense that anyone can have this problem, and anyone can use our solutions. They're globally applicable, whether in a slum in Mumbai or in downtown Toronto, you're using the fish, you're using the powder. But I do think that how we approach the markets is different in terms of issues such as pricing and sustainability, marketing strategy, and e-commerce."

As pandemic restrictions began to ease and international selling began to ramp up, Armstrong says that in some sense one could see him as the sales leader, but he argues that this is not the case. He points instead to team member Anne Pringle, who for the past few years has been guiding the NGO sales.

"I have the technical background," he says, "so I have that authority in the space around the efficacy in the data and the research. As well, especially in certain countries, the prestige of the position matters, the CEO meets with the CEO. But Anne did a lot of the work and put all the effort in to make it happen."

Looking again to the future, in January 2023 the company hired a new person to manage sales, and Pringle's role was shifted more to program management.

At that point, "we were in this position where we had so many existing programs that we wanted to scale. One person alone can't focus on those programs while growing and building out the pipeline. So the new hire can build out the pipeline, while Anne manages existing relationships, makes sure they're effective and successful, and then works to help them scale up."

As for the manufacturing side of the company, Armstrong says the team will continue to work with the partner in India. "We have a fantastic relationship with our partner, they are family owned, our values are aligned, and the quality is there. So I think it makes sense just to keep partnering and grow with them." The same firm in India is providing one of the ingredients for the powder, along with producing the iron fish, but the powder product itself will be assembled with other ingredients in Canada.

As for shipping and distribution, Armstrong says the company will continue to explore those issues. "Right now, it makes sense to do things through here in Canada, just due to the way we are facilitated through Amazon," he explains.

Another initiative Armstrong would like to explore in the coming years is in the area of diagnostics, where tools might be developed to assess iron levels without going the intrusive route of drawing blood. He points to tools such as watches that can monitor heartbeats or count steps.

"I'm very open," he says. "I'm very interested in collaboration or a partnership for the development of a simple diagnostic tool. Many experts believe iron deficiency is underdiagnosed globally. It's definitely a more serious problem in the developed world, or in high-income countries, than is believed, and right now the standard way people find out is a blood test by their doctor, but that takes time, is invasive, and in certain contexts is expensive.

"I would love a smartphone app or some form of tool that you can have at your own disposal where you would be able to look at your iron levels. If we can identify easily that you have a problem, we can recommend solutions for you. And then when you buy our solutions, you can use our tool to track the impact it's having."

Armstrong envisions a tool or device that would be able to assess the colour in one's blood cells, looking for a deeper red versus the paler red that would mean lower levels of iron.

"I have an Apple watch that can tell me all sorts of blood oxygen levels and other things in my body," he says, "and it does not require taking blood. So there are tools that already exist that are non-invasive. They're not incredibly accurate at this point, but it doesn't mean they can't become more accurate moving forward."

Armstrong says he doesn't see the business developing such a tool on its own, but instead imagines a possible strategic partnership with an established firm that could help develop a monitoring product that would meet Lucky Iron Fish's demands of rigour.

"That means partnering with a technical development firm, and there are companies that are building these tools now," he says. "We have to pay attention to the landscape and read the data. They're not there yet, but they'll continue to get there. And once we find one, we would want to look to partner with them."

Armstrong sees a range of paths to getting such a product to the marketplace, such as buying out the developers or possibly merging with them, or just simply establishing a commercial relationship. "How that ends up looking will depend on where we are as a business at the time when we would want to pull the trigger," he says.

As he looks to the past and the future, he explains that Lucky Iron Fish has been the first real "adult" job he has had, and he has embraced it enthusiastically.

"It's been definitely trial by fire, but I have put a system in place to make sure that I am the right person for the job," he recounts. "I have a very thorough review process with my board, and they believe in me, and I currently believe in me. But if a point ever comes where I'm outside of my depth and someone else with more experience could take us further, I would never let my vanity get in the way of the growth of the business. I'm currently in charge and leading the growth, but if a day comes when I just am not the right person, that will be my time to move on to my next adventure. I've never led a fifty-million-dollar corporation that's in seventy countries, for example. If we get to the point that I just don't know what I'm doing and the advice from the team and the system I put in place is that someone else could do a more effective job, I will listen to that."

He acknowledges that such an outcome is nowhere on the horizon at present, before adding, with a wry smile, "But I hope the fifty million is."

While the hope for those soaring financials may be off in the distance at present, there is a front-of-mind goal over the next five years for Armstrong, which is to become a recognized global leader of all things iron deficiency.

"When you think about the problem of iron deficiency, the brand name Lucky Iron Fish should immediately come to mind."

# Epilogue

# A Conversation About Mental Health and the Workplace

IT DOES SEEM incongruous to suggest that there could be any positives arising from the world's protracted battle with Covid-19. Perhaps it's not a benefit, but rather something inspired by the battle with the disease. That something is awareness. Specifically, an awareness of mental health challenges that have been brought to front of mind for people who have struggled to adapt to working remotely, or others who have had to use their entrepreneurial instincts to keep their businesses solvent and growing. And at the same time, business leaders have also realized the importance of keeping the mental health of their teams in mind.

Then, too, on a personal level, for individuals such as Armstrong and Darrell Schuurman of the CGLCC, recognizing, accepting and advocating for sexual rights is a constant backdrop for the discussion of mental health.

"From an entrepreneur's perspective, there are many challenges around mental health and well-being," Armstrong says. "There's obviously a Covid-19 angle to it because things have been much more amplified the past three years. I have participated in multiple group discussions with other founders and entrepreneurs. A recurring and very common theme is that entrepreneurs and leaders are really concerned about the mental health of their teams.

"And there's a lot more emphasis being put now on providing resources and support for team members. For Lucky Iron Fish, mental health days are encouraged if you need one. I am very cognizant of burnout and try to pay attention to not just the number of tasks everyone has, but their tone and the way that they're talking about their work. You can get a sense when things are becoming too much.

"One of the things that I learned through employee feedback from my performance review was even though we had these [mental health days] available for staff, they weren't taking them because I wasn't taking them. And as someone who sets the standard for the organization, if I'm not taking a mental health day, others don't want to be the first one to do it. I say, 'Don't work during your vacation,' but I work during my vacation, so other people feel that they have to do that. I heard that feedback, so I was the first one to take a mental health day — and I really needed one. It was a heavy period. I've stopped doing emails and things on my vacation."

Lucky Iron Fish team members do self-assessments of their performance, and that is how it emerged that they were reluctant to take those mental health days because Armstrong himself was not taking those days.

"I'm trying to set more boundaries so I can lead by example on that front. We now as a company provide apps for stress management. We have some executive coaching that some employees have taken advantage of. I'm doing it as well. So those things have been helpful. That was pre–Covid-19. Then you look at during Covid-19. Just looking at the staff who have kids, and when schools went to virtual for many months, you just see that they're trying to do their job and be teachers and caretakers. It's impossible to not have your plate be too full. It's really hard, and we've tried to find strategies and ways we can help out in those circumstances."

In a nebulous area such as mental health, there is no simple handbook to follow, and, with every organization being unique, they must adapt and adjust.

"We have not really zeroed in on mental health within our organization, so that is something we are looking at," Schuurman explains. "We are at least now having that conversation around mental health and its impact on our businesses.

"For queer individuals, Covid-19 has had an effect on our mental health, so we want our members to know we are there for them. In terms of staffing issues in the area of mental health, that is not unique to the 2SLGBTQI+ community. It's an issue for all businesses to be aware of with their teams and their challenges. As entrepreneurs, we need be aware of that, so we create events at the chamber. At the start, I thought team members would see it as something they were obliged to do, but the CGLCC team members love the weekly social."

Schuurman says with the CGLCC team itself, "there had absolutely been Covid-19 exhaustion. Like everyone, we had to limit who can come into the office. Covid-19 was hard on our team members' and chamber members' mental health."

Armstrong concurs, noting, "You're only as strong as your team, so if they're burning out, that's a huge risk to the organization."

On a personal level, he acknowledges he was facing burnout and doing nothing constructive to help recharge himself. He notes these issues were in play for him prior to Covid-19, but the pandemic thoroughly exacerbated the problem.

"You couldn't travel, vacations were spent locked down in your apartment," Armstrong says. "Your office was your living room. There's no escape. Things definitely got really worse with Covid-19, but it helped me realize that I had been allowing myself to get burned out before the pandemic."

In Armstrong's instance, he admits that there were telltale signs, such as difficulties concentrating, trouble sleeping, and a poor diet, leading to a lack of energy. A common theme in discussions among entrepreneurs running a startup is that there are so many risks and so many ways it can go sideways.

"Startups are generally running deficits. You're not making money, and you're surviving on investment capital," Armstrong explains. "You think regularly during the day about what happens if you go out of business. That kept me up for a couple of reasons. One was the fear for my staff. I've got people who put their trust in me and believe that we're going to do something, and they're going to be protected as employees. If we run out of money, and they can't afford their mortgages and their kids' meals, that is stressful and a challenge to mental health.

"Another piece is that my personal brand, my identity, is connected to this company. It was hard to not assume that if the company fails, I'm a failure. I think a lot of entrepreneurs feel that way. I actually did an executive coaching exercise on this where the coach said, 'Picture success, let's say you've been bought out. Tell me what you see.' We were having a party with the staff, and everyone was happy. The language was 'We did it, we worked together, we accomplished our goals, and we made this happen.' And then we were to visualize the opposite of that, what happens if it's bankrupt? My language was 'I failed. I didn't do it. I couldn't get this done.' The facilitator said, 'Why is it when it's a win, it's we, but if it's a loss, it's you?' I think a lot of entrepreneurs feel that way, where the weight of the entire organization is on their shoulders. It can cause a lot of stress and anxiety." And that means reverting to the issue of mental health concerns.

In addition to self-assessment, Armstrong has his own review where a committee interviews both board members and staff about how they feel he has performed.

"Feedback from the staff was they could tell I was burning out. I didn't get specific examples, but I think it was my attitude, my general demeanour, probably my appearance. You could see the stress on me. When I was honest with the team members that I needed to start focusing more on my own self-care, it wasn't a surprise to them, because they were the ones that saw it every day."

Those observations about his own challenges helped Armstrong take steps and implement policies to support the mental health of team members. And he says the steps were appreciated and the staff started engaging in those measures.

"There's always a bit of reluctance because everyone wants to come across as strong, so we need to open up more and talk more about the challenges that we face."

Lucky Iron Fish had to move to full virtual communications after the onslaught of Covid-19. Armstrong points out that before, when team members were in the office, one could better gauge how people were doing with respect to body language and other non-verbal signs.

But when they had to go the virtual route, "once you disconnect from a Zoom meeting, you don't know how they are, so I did more one-on-one check-ins. Once a month, once every couple of months, with everyone and just asked the questions, 'How's it going? What do you need? Is there anything I can do to make your life better?' Parents on the team acknowledged how stressful it was. In these meetings, kids would be in the background or climbing on them. You saw it happening in front of you.

"I believe that the best thing you can do for your organization is let your team become more empowered to move themselves up," Armstrong adds. "The opposite of that is you have people leave because they just can't handle the job and it's too stressful. That is a blow to the organization because you lose the institutional knowledge and bear the cost and time it takes to onboard someone. I focus on mental health because it's important, and it's something I have not done well in the past. But there's absolute organizational importance to doing it."

Armstrong argues that a firm's employees are its most important resource and investment, and to be genuinely looking out for the best interests of the business means making sure employees are "in the best place they can be. And that would include supporting mental health and being proactive around mental health challenges."

He points out that, among the many changes brought on by Covid-19, operating in a virtual environment meant there were few borders between a person's work life and their personal life, which made it harder for people to create space for themselves. Lucky Iron Fish team members tried to focus on that reality during the pandemic and have since maintained that focus as regular office work has resumed. In addition, company supervisors including Armstrong are encouraged to monitor the workloads of staff, "because burnout is real," he notes.

"Sometimes things are really stressful, and we just try our best to work through it and be supportive of one another. That's why one of the critical components for our weekly meetings is to focus on transparency about what is going on. So if one staff person's plate just seems incredibly full, other people are not going to pile on and make things worse. Instead, they dial it back a bit."

Armstrong acknowledges that some employees may not want to open up about issues affecting them because they worry it makes them look vulnerable.

"I also respect that it can be a very private matter, and you're under no obligation to tell a supervisor or your team if you're going through something like I was going through the past year with some personal life stuff," he says. "I understand, because I felt a little awkward bringing my personal life to the workplace."

The recognition that the issues involving mental health in the workplace are not being addressed is an indictment of the mental health support system, Armstrong says. He adds that Lucky Iron Fish has a reasonable health benefit plan that staff can use.

"Our health benefit plan is pretty good for a small business, but it's still not amazing," he says. "The big insurers don't provide very competitive plans. It's actually quite limited with respect to the plans that are available for us. I wish that mental health was better covered provincially rather than what we have."

He says that another possible challenge to mental health stability is somewhat unique to Lucky Iron Fish, in that team members who travel often find themselves in rough locations that remind them of the privilege they have.

"You will often have a feeling of guilt with respect to the hopelessness in some situations, and you're unsure what to do, because the problem can feel so daunting. It's a strain on your mental health," he explains. "I've heard this from staff who have travelled without me, and we've had some deep conversations — there have been some tears around it. Ultimately, what I try to reinforce is that we are a business trying to be one of many to provide solutions for disadvantaged populations, and our work does matter."

Armstrong offers himself as an example of the productivity costs of ignoring mental health issues spurred, for example, by burnout.

"Speaking personally, I'm a lot less productive when I'm going through a hard time," he says. "It's tough to find my motivation, I second-guess myself, and I'm constantly redoing things. You're distracted, perhaps not sleeping well, and that just carries into to your day. If you are not eating properly, you're not nourishing yourself."

Such a gloomy scenario can often prove costly for a business, but recognition of such outcomes is still very much emerging.

"I just don't understand," Armstrong muses. "Obviously if your employees are happy and healthy, they're going to be better, yet there was so much resistance to taking advantage of mental health supports. I think there's always a moral and an economic argument for addressing these issues."

As further evidence of the growing awareness of the impact of mental health issues on entrepreneurs and employees, we can turn to an extensive survey released in September 2022 by the Business Development Bank of Canada (BDC), which explored small- and medium-size enterprise owners' mental health and support. The findings clearly reflect the issues Schuurman and Armstrong point to. Here are some key BDC findings that relate to this discussion:

**1. Main sources of stress among entrepreneurs**
- Financial cash flow – 62%
- Economic recession – 51%
- Work/life balance – 48%
- Fear of loss/failure – 47%

**2. Personal coping strategies to address mental health issues**
- Finding quiet time to relax – 59%
- Exercise or physical activity – 53%
- Taking time off/vacation – 43%
- Seeking support from friends or family – 42%

**3. Seventy-three percent of respondents said the BDC should play a role in connecting entrepreneurs to mental health services. Services likely to be used:**
- Stress management training – 80%
- Online well-being educational content – 79%

- Virtual therapy – 73%
- Online cognitive behavioural therapy – 72%
- Peer support – 70%

## 4. Employees' mental health support

- 87% agreed that the mental health of their workforce is very important to the success of their business
- 72% said they placed a high priority on supporting the mental health of their employees
- The main sources of mental health issues among employees were financial problems, concerns over Covid-19, family/relationship changes, and client/customer demands
- In terms of ways to support employees' mental health, 55% pointed to flexible hours/schedule, 50% mentioned giving additional time when required, and 33% mentioned remote or hybrid work options

## 5. Top types of resources and supports needed

- Education for all employees on mental health
- Benefits coverage for psychological health care
- Support to develop a mental health strategy

Another take on the importance of businesses attending to mental health issues comes from another Canadian organization, the Centre for Addiction and Mental Health (CAMH), which has produced some intriguing findings.

"Work is the most stressful part of the day for 47 percent of all working Canadians," CAMH reports. "As Canada's largest mental health teaching hospital and a global leader in research, CAMH is uniquely positioned to catalyze and advance a nation-wide movement for better workplace mental health."

The organization coordinates Business Leaders for Mental Health Action, a philanthropic coalition of business leaders and companies committed to improving the psychological health and safety of employees and advocating for businesses to take action. Participants include an impressive list of leading companies that commit to taking a stand in support of better mental health, implementing mental health strategies, and aiming for better outcomes for people living with mental illness.

Some of the numbers CAMH reports are eye-opening. Citing other sources, the organization reports that every week, "half a million employees in Canada miss work due to mental illness. This amounts to roughly $6.3 billion in lost productivity every year. And, by 2041, it's estimated that mental illness will have cost the Canadian economy more than $2.5 trillion."

CAMH argues that "prioritizing and addressing mental health in the workplace is the right thing to do for your employees and for your bottom line. When done effectively, the potential impacts to your business include higher performance, lower absenteeism, and reduced disability costs."

In support of that argument, the organization points out that 30 percent of disability claims in Canada are due to mental illness, which accounts for 70 percent of all disability costs. The group also notes that the cost of disability leave for mental illness is about double the cost of leave due to physical illness.

And as no surprise, Covid-19 exacerbated issues around mental health. A survey done in early 2022 and reported by Postmedia looked at the mental health issues of more than 1,500 Canadian adults. Among its findings was that more than one-third (35 percent) of Canadian adults of all ages say their mental health is worse now than it was before the pandemic began.

Armstrong has personally benefitted from his executive coach in dealing with stress management and mental health. He has delved deeper into his connection with the CGLCC because it linked him with other entrepreneurs who are dealing with similar mental health issues. He has also begun to attend therapy, though he hastens to add that the program has less to do with work and is instead focused more on the trauma from the bullying he suffered through his youth.

"You have these core memories that influence the rest of your life, your decision-making, and how you interpret things," he says. "One of my memories is just being put down and made to feel worthless through the trauma of bullying. I have this lens when I'm making decisions or when I'm interpreting conversations or relationships, and it always seems to come back to me proving my worth. You have this huge part of your identity, which is your business, now being connected to your own self-worth. It can make the problem snowball. The therapy is to help me work through that."

Armstrong describes his own mental health status as the pandemic eased off as "medium," a description packed with variables.

Guided by his own experience, he advocates for mental health issues to be discussed to a greater extent across the community at large.

"I definitely think it should be talked about more, and I feel like I could use my experience," he says. "What's holding me back, and this is something my therapist said, is that I'm very self-aware of what my challenges and problems are, but I don't have the solutions — that's what's frustrating. I could talk about the importance of mental health, but I think where I would feel some resistance is that I don't have the answers yet."

He puts good stock in the input from Schuurman, who has himself been an entrepreneur for years.

"I'd be interested to see how Darrell's [Schuurman's] awareness and transparency around mental health and entrepreneurship have evolved over time. He does engage with multiple entrepreneurs through his job, and employers, too. How are big corporations dealing with mental health with their staff?" Armstrong wonders. With respect to awareness of LGBT issues and mental health, Schuurman says, "Yes, the two are very closely tied together. It's something many 2SLGBTQI+ people have to confront and struggle with. And you're always having to correct people with respect to what you might be struggling with.

"The first struggle is with self-realization and accepting yourself," Schuurman adds. "It takes a significant toll. You have to accept that you are queer and don't fit the world's view of normal. And then there is the coming out to other people, and that is ongoing. In conversations, we are engaging our members and trying to put a 2SLGBTQI+ lens on things."

From his own experience in coming to grips with his sexuality, Armstrong agrees with Schuurman's observations. "There are always the queer angles and how 2SLGBTQI+ communities deal with it," he says. "I'm not trying to paint everyone with the same brush, but if you've experienced trauma in your life, which I think a lot of queer people have, there's that added layer of mental health challenges from that perspective that can change the way you view things.

"I think back to my lowest points in high school, where I was in the hospital under supervision, having tried to take my own life, and just feeling like that was the end and there was no future, and I am amazed that just a decade later how much things had improved. You realize there is hope, and you can use that pain from the past as fuel to try to drive change. I wish I had an opportunity to go back in time and talk to my younger self, but I don't. But I do have the opportunity to tell the story for other young people who might be facing similar struggles."

# Appendix I

# Awards and Honours for Gavin Armstrong and LIFe

## Gavin Armstrong

**2011:** First Canadian to receive the William Jefferson Clinton Hunger Leadership Award for international work against hunger

**2012:** Inaugural recipient of the Michaëlle Jean Emergency Hunger Relief Award

**2013:** Guelph's Mayor Award of Excellence

**2015:** Conscious Company Magazine, featured as 1 of the 17 Rising Social Entrepreneurs of the Year

**2016:** *Forbes*'s 30 Under 30, Social Entrepreneur category

**2016:** Fulbright scholar at Auburn University

**2016:** The Town & Country 50, The Top Philanthropists of 2016

**2016:** University of Guelph Alumni Medal of Achievement

**2016:** Youngest recipient of the Social Innovator of the Year Award, Lewis Institute at Babson College in Massachusetts

**2017:** Muhammad Ali Humanitarian Award

**2017:** Social Entrepreneur of the Year, Ernst & Young (Canada)

**2018:** Successfully pitched Lucky Iron Fish on CBC's *Dragons' Den*

**2019:** Small Business Leader of the Year, Canada's 2SLGBTQI+ Chamber of Commerce

**2021:** Top 50 Changemakers, *Globe and Mail Report on Business*

## LIFe

**2015:** Cannes Lion Health Festival: Gold (Social and Health Impact)

**2015:** Cannes Lion Innovation Festival: Grand Prix (Product Design), Gold (Packaging), Gold (Public Relations), Silver (Activation)

**2015:** Clio Advertising Awards: Gold (Product), Gold (Innovation), Silver (Public Relations), Bronze (Design)

**2015:** Clio Health Care Awards: Grand Prix (Advertiser of the Year); Gold (Innovation); Gold (Design); Silver (Engagement/ Experimental); Silver (Direct Engagement)

**2015:** Design for Asia Grand Award

**2015:** Edison Innovation Award, Silver

# Appendix II

# Herb Shoveller's Publications, Awards, and Honours

*Go to School, You're a Little Black Boy* (2006), Lincoln Alexander's autobiography with Herb Shoveller, led to a subsequent documentary, *A Linc in Time*, released in 2010.

*Ryan and Jimmy and the Well in Africa That Brought Them Together* (2006)

**2006:** Book of the Year Award, ForeWord Magazine, short-listed

**2006:** Disney Adventures Book Award, winner

**2006:** Parents' Choice Recommended, winner

**2007:** Alberta Children's Rocky Mountain Book Award, short-listed

**2007:** Carol D. Reiser Award, Metro Atlanta Corporate Volunteer Council, winner

**2007:** Diamond Willow Award, Saskatchewan Young Readers' Choice, short-listed

**2007:** Information Book Award, Children's Literature Roundtables of Canada, short-listed

**2007:** International Book Award, The Society of School Librarians International, winner

**2007:** Norma Fleck Award, Canadian Children's Book Centre, short-listed

**2007:** Notable Books for a Global Society, International Reading Association, winner

**2007:** Notable Social Studies Trade Books for Young People, CBC, short-listed

**2007:** Skipping Stones Honor Award, Skipping Stones Magazine, winner

**2008:** Silver Birch Award, Ontario Library Association, short-listed

# Acknowledgements

### From Gavin Armstrong

First and foremost, I would like to thank Dr. Christopher Charles. Your innovative thinking and dedication to helping others established the foundations that we work from today.

Dr. Alastair Summerlee has been a teacher, mentor, grammar police officer, and friend. Thank you for believing in me when I did not.

Thank you to everyone who believed in the Lucky Iron Fish, including the researchers, NGO partners, investors, advisers, and customers. You helped take this simple idea and turn it into a global success.

Thank you to my family who have always encouraged and supported me, even during dark times.

There is a profound power in friendship, and without the love and support of my chosen family I wouldn't be here today. Through laughter and tears, thank you for everything that you do. Your simple acts of kindness have truly meant the world to me.

And finally, thank you to the entire Lucky Iron Fish team, past and present. Without your hard work, compassion, and commitment to our mission, this little fish would not be where it is today. I cannot wait to see where we take this next.

To the reader, no matter how daunting the challenge may seem, never underestimate the power of one. One person has the power to create a ripple that could end up changing the world.

## From Herb Shoveller

I am eternally grateful for the encouragement and support from family, immediate and extended, and friends to continue to pursue my writing and editing interests.

# Index

# Index

# Index

# About the Authors

Dr. Gavin Armstrong is the award-winning founder and CEO of Lucky Iron Fish Enterprise, a company dedicated to alleviating iron deficiency globally by using simple health innovations. Armstrong was named one of *Forbes*'s 30 Under 30. He also won the support of two Dragons on the CBC's *Dragons' Den*. He lives in Toronto.

Herb Shoveller spent twenty-five years in journalism before starting an independent writing and editing business. Among his projects have been the autobiography of Lincoln Alexander, the autobiography of union leader Lynn Williams, and a young readers book, *Ryan and Jimmy*. He lives in Cambridge, Ontario.

# About Lucky Iron Fish
# Enterprise (LIFe)

LUCKY IRON FISH Enterprise (LIFe) is a social enterprise dedicated to treating and preventing iron deficiency, which is the world's largest nutritional deficiency. Iron deficiency negatively impacts one out of three individuals (over two billion people) around the planet, predominantly women and children, especially those living in poverty. Signs and symptoms of iron deficiency include dizziness, fatigue, headaches and fainting, reduced cognitive development, and can even lead to death. It is estimated that 40 percent of maternal deaths are linked to iron deficiency anemia, and children who suffer from iron deficiency have reduced performance in school. Iron deficiency is estimated to contribute to a $110 billion annual global GDP loss, and in low- to middle-income countries it is estimated that iron deficiency contributes to a 20 percent loss of earned income among women. LIFe was founded in 2012 by Dr. Gavin Armstrong in Guelph, Ontario, and is now headquartered in Toronto, Ontario.